It gives me great pleasure to provide introductory remarks for Dr. John Philpott's *Gourmet Meals That Will Melt In Your Mouth.* I have known the Author for many years both as a patient and friend. During our first professional encounter I found that many of his teeth had a very poor long-term prognosis, and felt it was only a matter of time until he would transition to complete dentures.

It was during this time that John brought me many interesting and very delicious recipes, along with his special sauces and herbal vinegars, which definitely delight the palate.

Out of the Author's own experience of transitioning from natural teeth to dentures, he has written a very fine and much needed cookbook to assist others who find themselves in this unfortunate situation.

This cookbook fills a void and addresses a question I am asked daily, "Doctor after I lose my teeth, how and what will I eat?" *Gourmet Meals That Will Melt In Your Mouth* answers these questions. Regardless of your dental status, it is my desire that you will enjoy the gourmet meals contained in this book which was written by a very knowledgeable and respected Author.

Charles E. Conklin, Jr., DDS

Dedication

To the dental professionals of North America. This is a heart-felt thank you for performing an often-frustrating task (we the patients often do not live up to our part of the partnership).

I salute you for your dedication, warmth and professionalism.

Introduction

The purpose of this cookbook is to acquaint you, the reader, with cooking techniques designed to deal with the loss of teeth, and is designed for you. This is a gradual process, but an increasingly traumatic experience up to the time that the last teeth are extracted.

It is not a happy experience to be losing your teeth. It was for me a very traumatic sequence of events, where favorite dishes became progressively more difficult to eat. The following eleven chapters are presented with hopes that they will help you cope with your situation, as did I.

Importantly, these are all original recipes. Suggestions are provided at the end of each chapter for recipes that can be found elsewhere, but preserve the mission of this book.

The good news is that you will eventually get used to your dentures and be able once more to eat anything that you choose. The bad news is that during this transition you will initially experience the same trauma that I did unless you use the recipes contained herein to help bridge the gap.

I refused to give up fine foods throughout this process, and told myself that I would not be forced into a diet of liquid supplements and (dread!) baby food. This cookbook is about how to deal with a dental problem, and still eat like royalty. The idea of eating strained peas and carrots along with a glass of fine wine is most unwelcome!

The format here is casual, so do not expect expensive photographs and the like. Our goal is to make this cookbook affordable to all. You are probably spending much of your discretionary income at the dentist's office, a most necessary expense.

These recipes helped me to get through some very tough times. I hope that they will help you as well. I close with the admonition to not let what you are going through get the best of you; instead, let your challenge be dealt with in a most delightful way.

Some important guidelines are:

1. Use only the best ingredients, as the savings on "bargain" items is not worth the loss of quality, and they tend to be tougher.
2. Never, ever overcook any item, it also makes them tougher.
3. Chicken, fish, and shellfish are particularly bad when overcooked. Sauté them lightly, then set aside, make your sauce, then re-add the meat about 2 minutes prior to serving.
4. With pork it is best to stick it in your freezer for several weeks (2 weeks at –20° F., longer if your freezer temperature is higher and less if colder). This is called "certified pork", and may actually be eaten raw with no danger of trichina.
5. Vegetables should not be cooked until they are "gray".
6. It is OK to boil water, but not soups or sauces.

Bon Appetit!

John E. Philpott, Ph.D.

Contents

Presented in Grateful Appreciation

for the contribution made by

𝕵𝖔𝖍𝖓 𝕰. 𝕻𝖍𝖎𝖑𝖕𝖔𝖙𝖙, 𝕭. 𝕾., 𝕸. 𝕽. 𝕰., 𝕻𝖍. 𝕯.

to the Scientific Program of the

Fifty-Eighth Annual Session of the

Greater New York Dental Meeting
1982

General Chairman

Secretary-Treasurer

Chapter

1

Certain ingredients are the keys to great meals. Coming to mind are Glacé de Viande, Clarified Butter, and the immortal Roux.

When using hot spices, follow the "Goldilocks Rule": not too hot, not too cold, but "just right". Do it to your taste. My experience is that the further south one lives, the hotter the guests like the meal. When cooking in North Dakota, you might tactfully ask your guests how they like it. Cooking in Laredo, Texas, the answer is a "no brainer", they like it so hot that Tabasco sauce is called tame. Some of my salsas, Salsa Mansa and Furious Yellow are big hits there. These same salsas in New England would be deemed to be lethal.

Know your guests well. What I like to do is to show them the cookbook in advance and ask them what they would like. Crab Louis is delicious, but don't make the mistake of serving it to a Muslim friend, like I did. This chapter includes ingredients which cover the entire taste spectrum.

One final tip: when serving an Indian Curry, a good companion would be a yogurt, mint, cucumber sauce. The "cool" with the "hot" is a well-appreciated touch.

BLACKENING POWDER

Ingredients:
- 3 Tbs. Hungarian Paprika
- 2 Tbs. Sea Salt
- 1 Tbs. Garlic Powder
- 1 Tbs. Onion Powder
- 1½ Tsp. Cayenne
- 1½ Tsp. Black Pepper
- 1½ Tsp. White Pepper
- 1 Tsp. Thyme
- 1 Tsp. Oregano
- 1 Tsp. Basil
- 1 Tsp. Bay Leaf, Powdered
- 1 Tsp. Chervil

Directions:
Mix all ingredients together and store in air tight container until needed.

CAJUN 12 SPICE POWDER

Ingredients:

1 Tbs. Each:
- Basil
- Black Pepper,
- Chinese Mustard
- Gumbo Filé
- Garlic Powder
- Salt
- Sugar
- Thyme
- White Pepper

1/2 Tbs. Each:
- Ground Bayleaf
- Coriander
- Powdered Horseradish
- Hungarian Paprika
- Cayenne Pepper

Directions:
Mix in a bowl and store in a sealed container until needed.

CAJUN 14 SPICE POWDER

Ingredients:

2 Tbs. Each:
- Garlic Powder
- Onion Powder
- Thyme
- Cayenne
- White Pepper

1 Tbs. Each:
- Dry Mustard
- Black Pepper
- Oregano
- Basil
- Cumin
- Gumbo Filé
- Celery Leaf
- Chervil
- Powdered Bay Leaf

Directions:

Combine all ingredients, and store in air-tight container until needed.

CHILI OIL
(Oil of Olé)

Ingredients:

2 Cups Sesame Oil
2 Cups Dried Red Peppers, (ideally, chilis Pequines), Chopped
Powdered Cumin
Dried Cilantro Leaf
Powdered Garlic

Directions:

Heat sesame oil hot enough to make a piece of dried pepper "dance" on the surface. Remove from heat and add chopped peppers, cumin, cilantro, and garlic to oil. Return to stove over low heat and allow to cook for several hours. Strain through a coffee filter and bottle.

This ruby-colored oil has many purposes. Use 1 tablespoon per pound of meat as a marinade for many Mexican, Thai, and Szechuan dishes. This preparation is also of pharmaceutical interest. For a "counter-irritant", omit the spices, cumin, garlic, and cilantro, and use the "pure extract".

CLARIFIED BUTTER

Ingredients:

> 2 Pounds Unsalted Butter

Directions:

Place butter in saucepan over low heat until melted. Allow to sit until it separates into three layers: foam on the top, a clear center, and solids on the bottom. Carefully skim the foam off of the top. Next, carefully pour the clarified center layer from the solids on the bottom. Some filter through cheesecloth, but careful pouring will serve the same purpose. The results are Clarified Butter. You may wish to refrigerate it in a container; however, it will keep excellently at room temperature for quite a long time.

Many recipes call for Clarified Butter without giving an explanation as to just what it is. It goes by other names: Ghee and Ghi. It is a basic ingredient in hotter climates. Most importantly for the chef, it does not burn in the frying pan like regular butter does. It has legendary powers to keep, even at room temperature for a long time. Butter has light solids and heavy solids that both can become rancid. Ghee eliminates these. Use Clarified Butter in place of oil whenever you can, as it imparts a noble flavor to whatever you cook. This is wonderful stuff, and a key to fine cuisine. Use it in place of cooking oils, and in its own right in place of regular butter.

CLASSIC CURRY POWDER

Ingredients:
> 2 Tbs. of Each:
>> Chili Powder
>> Hungarian Paprika
>> Turmeric
>
> 1 Tbs. of Each:
>> Coriander
>> Onion Powder
>> Mint
>> Cayenne
>
> 2 Tsp. of Each:
>> Cumin
>> Cinnamon
>> Allspice
>
> 1 Tsp. of Each:
>> Dry Mustard
>> Dill Weed
>> Garlic Powder
>> Fenugreek, Powdered
>> Cloves, Powdered
>> Ginger, Powdered
>
> $^1/_2$ Tsp. of Each:
>> Bay Leaf, Powdered
>> White Pepper
>
> Pinch of Saffron

Directions:
> Mix all ingredients thoroughly and store in an airtight container until needed.

GARAM MASALA
(Mild Curry Powder)

Ingredients:

    1½ Tbs. Coriander seeds
    1 Tbs. Cumin Seeds
    1 Tsp. Black Pepper
    1 Tsp. Mace
    ¼ Tsp. Cinnamon
    ¼ Tsp. Cloves
    ⅛ Tsp. Green Cardamom Seeds.
    ⅛ Tsp. Bay Leaf Powder

Directions:

1. Finely grind all ingredients.
2. Mix thoroughly and store in an airtight container for at least 3 days before use. Yield: about ¼ Cup.
3. Use this mild curry powder in northern Indian dishes, and try it with other cuisine.

GLACÉ DE VIANDE

Ingredients:

10 7" Beef Marrow Bones, slit longitudinally. Remove marrow from all but 4 halves, and save for other purposes (eg. Bordelaise Sauce!)

2 Cloves Garlic, crushed	2 Dried Cloves
2 Tbs Chicken Boullion Powder	1 Cup Onions, Chopped
1 Tsp Thyme	½ Cup Carrots, Chopped
1 Tsp Bay Leaf Powder	½ Cup Celery, Chopped
1 Tbs Parsley	3 Gallons Water

Directions:

Add all ingredients to 20 quart pot and simmer for 3-4 hours. Strain and re-add liquid only to pot, skimming off any solids on top, and avoiding those on bottom when pouring. Simmer, uncovered until reduced to about 3-4 pints of Glacé. Separate into 8 containers and freeze until needed. This is the ingredient that separates the 5-star from the 4-star restaurants.

MADRAS 14 SPICE MIXTURE
(Curry Powder)

Ingredients:

    1 Tsp. Of Each:
- Cumin
- Coriander
- Fenugreek
- Ginger
- Mustard Powder
- Cayenne

    $1/2$ Tsp. Of Each:
- Cardamom
- Turmeric
- Cinnamon
- Celery Powder

    $1/4$ Tsp. Of Each:
- Powdered Bay Leaf
- Powdered Cloves
- Wasabe Powder
- White Pepper

Directions:

Mix all ingredients thoroughly and store in air tight container until needed.

MAKING A ROUX

Ingredients:

    $1/4$ Cup Clarified Butter
    $1/4$ Cup Flour

Directions:

Place clarified butter in a skillet and heat very hot. Add flour, tilting pan to mix thoroughly. Be careful here to use a long spoon, as the water in the flour will cause spattering (Paul Prudhomme calls a roux "Cajun Napalm"!!). Cook to desired color, and use in soufflés, or other dishes that call for world-class thickeners. This, too, is a basic ingredient for many meals.

NAM PRIK
(Thai Curry Paste)

Ingredients:

6 Fresh Green Thai Peppers, stemmed
1 Tbs. Fresh Shallots, peeled
1 Tbs. Lemon Grass (lower part)
1 Tbs. Cilantro
1 Tbs. Garlic, peeled
1 Tbs. Macadamia Nuts, or Brazil Nuts, finely chopped
1 Tsp. Coriander Seeds
$^1\!/_2$ Tsp. Sea Salt
$^1\!/_2$ Tsp. Nam Pla (Fish Sauce)
$^1\!/_2$ Tsp. Kha (Galanga) or Ginger
$^1\!/_4$ Tsp. Black Peppercorns
3 Tsp. Soybean Oil
1 Tsp. Sesame Oil

Directions:

1. Add all ingredients to blender and mix thoroughly.
2. Green Thai peppers are hotter than the mature red ones. This is VERY hot!
3. Use in Thai, Southern Indian, and certain Vietnamese dishes.

Chapter
2

Soups are always a great opening to a grand meal, along with salads. They can also be a meal unto themselves. Soups can be made cold for warm weather (e.g.: Gaspacho) or hot and heavy for cold weather (e.g.: Borscht).

Certain soups are legendary in their taste. In all, they belong to any great meal. Experiment with this wonderful class of fine cuisine.

BLACK BEAN SOUP

Ingredients:
> 1/2 Pound Black Beans, rinsed
> 2 1/2 Quarts Water
> 1/2 Tsp. Salt
> 1 Cup Glacé de Viande (or 1-10 1/2 Oz. Can beef gravy)
> 1 Medium Onion, chopped
> 2 Cloves Garlic, chopped
> 1 Carrot, peeled and chopped
> 1 Stalk Celery, chopped
> 1 1/2 Cups Clarified Butter
> 1 Tbs. Balsamic Vinegar
> 1 Tsp. Each: Bay Leaf Powder, Chervil, Parsley, Thyme, and
>   Dark Brown Sugar
> 1/2 Tsp. Black Pepper
> 1 Cup Cubed (1/2 inch) Ham (Canned or Fresh)
> 2 Tbs. Dry Sherry
> 1/4 Cup Sour Cream

Directions:
1. Boil beans in salted water for 5 minutes. Cover and let stand for 1 1/2 hours.
2. Sauté veggies in clarified butter until limp, but not browned.
3. Combine vegetables with beans, add vinegar and spices. Simmer for 2 hours.
4. Add ham and sherry 15 minutes before serving.
5. Serve topped with sour cream.
6. A good Riesling goes well with this, as does a Chardonnay.

BORSCHT

Ingredients:

A. 1¹/₂ Pounds Beef Chuck
   ¹/₂ Pound Lean Pork
   ¹/₄ Pound Ham, finely chopped
   ¹/₄ Cups Beef Marrow
   1 Cup Glacé de Viande (or, include split bones when boiling meat)

B. 4 Cups Chopped Cabbage
   6 Beets, boiled, skinned and grated
   2 Medium Potatoes, finely chopped
   1 Stalk Celery, finely chopped
   ¹/₂ Cup Carrot, finely chopped
   2 Medium Tomatoes, peeled, seeded and finely chopped
   1 Tbs Chopped Fresh Parsley

C. 2 Tbs. Vinegar
   2 Tsp Brown Sugar
   2 Tsp Sea Salt
   1 Tsp Dill Weed
   ¹/₂ Tsp Black Pepper
   ¹/₂ Tsp Bay Leaf Powder

D. Sour Cream
   Clarified Butter
   6 Cups Water

Directions:

1. Boil beef and pork in salted water. Remove, but reserve broth. Add to broth, glacé and marrow. Simmer for 1¹/₂ hours. Shred meat when cooled, and add back to broth.
2. Boil beets, remove skins, and shred. Add to broth.
3. Sauté cabbage, leeks, carrots, celery, parsley, tomatoes, and potatoes in clarified butter, and add to broth.
4. Add vinegar, sugar, pepper, dill weed, and bay leaf. Simmer for 2 hours, covered. Maintain volume with added water.
5. Add ham chunks 5 minutes prior to serving.
6. Serve, topped with a tablespoon of sour cream per serving.

CAJUN CONCH SOUP

Ingredients:

Conch Meat: 13 oz. of the canned, 16 oz. of the fresh (or alternative)
1 Medium Onion
1 Stalk Celery
2 Cloves Garlic
2 oz. Fresh Spinach
1 oz. Fresh Parsley (stems removed)
8 oz. Can Tomato Sauce
10$\frac{1}{2}$-oz. Can Beef Broth
1 Tbs. Lemon Juice
3 Tbs. Sherry
2 Tbs. Flour (mix into beef broth)
$\frac{1}{2}$ Tsp. Anchovy Paste
3 Tbs. Butter
1 Tbs. Baking Soda
1 Tbs. Cajun 12 Spice Mixture (add more if from Louisiana!)

Directions:

Parboil conch slices in baking soda for about 5 minutes (also applies to Abalone and Turtle Meat). Remove, drain and slice into 1/8" strips. Sauté in butter, then add chopped vegetables and sauté for 10 more minutes. Add Tomato Sauce and stir for 5 minutes. Add remaining ingredients, stir, then cover and let simmer for several hours (the longer the better). Make up for lost volume by adding water.

Enjoy with a good Gewürztraminer, ideally from late picked grapes.

CRAB AND ASPARAGUS SOUP

Ingredients:
>   2 Quarts Water, Lightly Salted
>   1 Chicken Carcass
>   1 Tbs. Dried Chicken Bouillon
>   2 Tbs. Cornstarch, if needed
> $^1/_2$ Pound Lump Crabmeat, preferably Dungeness, picked over
>   1 12 to 15 oz. Can White Asparagus, cut into thirds, plus liquid
>   2 Shallots, chopped
>   1 Clove Garlic, crushed
> $1^1/_2$ Tbs. Crushed Ginger
>   2 Tbs. Sesame Oil
>   1 Tbs. Sea Salt
> $^1/_4$ Tsp. Freshly Ground Black Pepper
>   2 Tsp. Fish Sauce
>   1 Tsp. Maggi Sauce
>   2 Jumbo Eggs, Whipped in a Cup
>   1 Tbs. Dry Sherry
>   Cilantro Sprigs for Garnish

Directions:
1. Bring chicken and bouillon to a boil, and simmer for $1^1/_2$ hours. Skim off foam and strain (reserve: gravy, and possibly thicken with cornstarch). Discard bones.
2. Cook garlic, ginger, and shallots in oil.
3. Add crabmeat, fish sauce, Maggi sauce, and pepper, and stir-fry for 2 minutes. Add asparagus.
4. Add water, gravy, asparagus liquid, and mix and simmer for 2-5 minutes.
5. Stir in eggs and sherry.
6. Serve, topped with Cilantro.
7. A good Chardonnay is appropriate with this meal.

Serving Suggestions:
>   Appetizer: Spring Rolls   Salad: Tiger Cry
>   Dessert: Coconut Milk Ice Cream, with Mint

Comments:
This is a combination of both Vietnamese and Thai cuisine. I consider it to be most compatible. Have a variety of sauces available for the spring rolls: Hoisin, Sweet & Sour, Hot Mustard, etc.

CREAM OF LEEK SOUP

Ingredients:

2 Leeks, trimmed, cleaned, and chopped into about 2"
    lengths (3 Cups)
1 Medium Potato, peeled, sliced, boiled in 3 cups water, then
    mashed
$1/2$ Cup Heavy Cream
$1/4$ Cup Ham, finely chopped and browned in clarified butter
2 Tsp Dried Thyme
$1/4$ Tsp Each: Cayenne, White Pepper
1 Tbs Sea Salt
1 Tsp Each: Powdered Bay Leaf, Parsley, Chervil
2 Tbs Dry Sherry

Directions:

1. Grind leeks in blender in 3 batches with 1 cup water each
   time, then add to a Dutch Oven (or other covered pot). Add
   garlic, potatoes, ham and spices. Cook for several hours,
   maintaining volume at about 2 quarts by occasionally adding
   water.
2. About 15 minutes prior to serving, add cream and sherry, and
   cover.

CUCUMBER AND LEEK SOUP
(A Midsummer Day's Dream)

Ingredients:

2 Cups Cucumber, peeled,
    seeded and chopped
2 Cups Chopped Leeks (white portion)
1 Cup Chicken Broth
$1/2$ Cup Heavy Cream

1 Tbs. Fresh Parsley
1 Tsp. Chopped Garlic
$1/2$ Tsp. Sea Salt
$1/4$ Tsp. White Pepper
$1/4$ Tsp. Cayenne

Directions:

1. Add cucumber, garlic and parsley to blender and emulsify.
   Pour into a 2-quart container.
2. Add leeks, chicken broth, cream, and remaining ingredients
   to blender and emulsify. Add to cucumber; mix thoroughly.
3. Refrigerate for 2 hours and serve cold.
4. A well-chilled Chardonnay is called for here.

CREOLE CHICKEN & RICE SOUP

Ingredients:

    A. 1 Pound Chicken Tenders, tendon removed, and chopped into small pieces.
        1 Tbs. Clarified Butter

    B. 2 Plum Tomatoes, peeled, seeded and chopped.
        $1/4$ Cup Green Bell Pepper, seeded and chopped
        $1/4$ Cup Red Bell Pepper, seeded and chopped
        $1/4$ Cup Chopped Onion
        $1/4$ Cup Peas
        $1/4$ Cup Kernel Corn
        1 Tbs. Clarified Butter.

    C. 1 Quart of Chicken Broth
        $1/2$ Tsp. Tabasco Sauce

    D. $1/4$ Tsp. Each:
            Chervil
            Basil
            Thyme
            Bay Leaf Powder
        $1/8$ Tsp. Each:
            Dill Weed
            Gumbo Filé
            Sea Salt
            White and Cayenne Pepper

    E. $1/2$ Cup Cooked Rice (ideally "Wild Pecan Rice")

Directions:

1. Lightly brown chicken in clarified butter. Set aside.
2. Brown the peppers and onion in clarified butter. Then add remaining vegetables.
3. Add chicken broth, seasonings and rice. Simmer for 1 hour. Add chicken shortly before serving.
4. Serve with a nice dry Chardonnay.

FRENCH ONION SOUP

Ingredients:

3 Large Onions, thinly sliced	1 Tsp. Each of Black and
1 Clove Garlic, Crushed	White Pepper
1/2 Stick Butter	1/2 Tsp. Nutmeg
2 Beef Bouillon Cubes	1/4 Tsp. Kitchen Bouquet
4+ Cups Boiling Water	Gruyere Cheese, Thinly Sliced
1/2 Cup Chablis	Sliced French Bread, toasted

Directions:

1. Brown sliced onion and garlic in butter until limp.
2. Cover with boiling water and dissolved boullion cubes.
3. Add peppers, nutmeg and Kitchen Bouquet.
4. Simmer for at least 30 minutes, then add wine. Continue cooking for another 30 minutes.
5. Place toasted bread slices on bottom of soup bowls.
6. Pour soup over bread and top with sliced cheese.
7. Place bowls in moderate oven until cheese melts.

GAZPACHO*

Ingredients:

2-15 Oz. Cans of Tomato Sauce	2 Tsp. Each: Red Wine Vinegar,
2 Medium Onions**	Extra Virgin Olive Oil
2 Cloves Garlic	1 Tsp. Each: Sea Salt, Lime Juice
1 1/2 Cups Cucumber**, peeled and seeded	1/2 Tsp. Tabasco Sauce (more, if Texan)
1 Bell Pepper**, seeded	1/4 Tsp. Black Pepper
1/2 Cup Plain Bread Crumbs	

Garnish:

Fresh Cilantro Leaf or Plain Croutons
Chopped Onion, Cucumber, and Bell Pepper

Directions:

Place all items in a blender, and liquefy. Set aside at room temperature for 2 hours, then place in refrigerator to chill. Add Garnish before serving.

*Known in 1836 as Gaspacho in Virginia, and Gaspachy Salad in Florida.
**Set aside a small portion of these items and finely chop to add as a garnish.

IRISH STEW

Ingredients:

$^3/_4$ Pounds Lamb Neck Bones

$^3/_4$ Pounds Spare Ribs

1 Quart Water

1 Can Beer

$^1/_2$ Tsp. Sea Salt

3 Strips Cooked Bacon, Chopped

1 Medium Onion, Chopped (about $1^1/_2$ Cups)

$2^1/_2$ Cups Cabbage, Finely Chopped

$^1/_4$ Cup Celery, Chopped

$^1/_4$ Cup Carrot, Chopped

4 Oz. Raw Potato Balls (~ $^3/_4$" Diam.)

3-4 Tbs. Clarified Butter

$^1/_2$ Tsp. Dill Seed

$^1/_2$ Tsp. Mace

$^1/_4$ Tsp. Black Pepper

1 Shot Irish Whiskey, or 2 Tbs. Dry Sherry

Directions:

1. Boil the bones in water, beer, and salt until the meat is easily removed from the bones. Reserve liquid, Add separated meat and chopped bacon to reserved liquid. Simmer lightly.

2. Sauté vegetables in clarified butter. Add to meat and simmer. Add Spices. Add Whiskey or Sherry just prior to serving.

OYSTER CHOWDER

Ingredients:

>12 Oz. Fresh Oysters and Oyster Liquor
>1 Potato, cubed
>1 Stalk Celery, Chopped
>1 Shallot, Chopped
>2 Cloves Garlic, Crushed
>1¼ Cups Canned Corn
>1 Carrot, Chopped
>1 Tsp. Chervil
>1 Tsp. Tarragon
>2 Tbs. Flour
>¼ Tsp. White Pepper
>¼ Tsp. Black Pepper
>¼ Tsp. Cayenne Pepper
>¼ Pound Butter (clarified, unsalted)
>½ Tsp. Sea Salt
>1½ Tbs. Chopped Parsley or Chives
>1 pint Cream
>1 Tbs. Sherry

Directions:

1. Boil potato, celery, carrot, shallots and corn in 1 quart salted water.
2. Add cream and oyster liquor. Bring to light boil.
3. Make a roux with 2 Tbs. butter and 2 Tbs. flour. Add to boiling mixture (above), stirring until thickened.
4. Sauté oysters in ¼ cup butter until edges curl. Add to above. Add sherry.
5. Place in serving bowls and garnish with either parsley or chives.
6. Serve with a Chardonnay.

MISO SOUP

Ingredients:

1 Cup White Miso added to 2 Quarts of Soup Stock
(or use Dashi), dissolve, and set aside.
2 Green Onion Tops, cut into narrow strips
6 Oz. Tofu, cut into $^1/_2$" cubes
$^1/_2$ Sheet Nori, cut into 12 pieces
2 Tbs. Fresh (or reconstituted) Shiitake Mushrooms, chopped
2 Tbs. Mirin (or Sake)

Directions:

1. Combine ingredients except Miso and divide among 4 bowls.
2. Heat Miso and Stock (recipe follows) on stove, then pour over the mix into bowls.

MISO SOUP STOCK

Ingredients:

5 Cups Water
1 Tbs. Fish Sauce (Nam Pla)
1 Tsp. Maggi Sauce
$^1/_2$ Tbs. Rice Vinegar
$^1/_2$ Sheet Nori, cut into 8 pieces
$^1/_4$ Cup Shrimp Shells or Fish Bones
2 Cubes Chicken Bouillon

Directions:

1. Combine all ingredients and simmer for 1 hour, then strain.
2. Re-add to pan and reduce volume to 2 quarts.
3. Combine with Miso, heat, and add to bowls with other ingredients.

REAL TEXAS CHILI

Ingredients:

      1 to 1½ Pounds Diced Sirloin (or better: Venison!)
      2 Tsp. Sea Salt
      1½ Tsp. Coarse Black Pepper
      2 Tbs. Extra Virgin Olive Oil
      2 Medium Onions, Chopped
      4 Cloves Garlic, Crushed
      2 Red Bell Peppers, Chopped

      2 Tbs. Each: Chili Powder, Cumin, Oregano
      ½ Tbs. Cilantro
      ½ Tsp. Basil
      28-32 Oz. Canned Tomatoes
      2 Tbs. Worcestershire Sauce
      1 Tsp. Tabasco Sauce (Bold: Habanero Sauce!)
      1 Cup Still Beer

Directions:

      Brown the sirloin or venison in olive oil, adding salt and pepper. Remove meat and set aside. Add onions, garlic, and peppers to pan and brown. Re-add meat and all other ingredients and simmer, uncovered, for at least 3 hours. Maintain desired volume with added still beer.

SPLIT PEA SOUP

Ingredients:

A. 1 pound Green Split Peas
   2½ Quarts Water
   1 Tsp. Sea Salt

B. 1 Cup Leeks, chopped
   ½ Cup Celery (with leaves), chopped
   2 Cloves Garlic, chopped
   1½ Tbs. Extra Virgin Olive Oil
   2 Chicken Bouillon Cubes in 1 cup boiling water

C. ½ Tsp. Chervil
   ½ Tsp. Dry Mustard
   ½ Tsp. White Pepper
   ½ Tsp. Cayenne Pepper
   ¼ Tsp. Thyme Powder
   ¼ Tsp. Bay Leaf Powder

D. ½ Cup Ham (or Pastrami), finely shredded

E. Dry Sherry

Directions:

1. Pick over split peas, rinse and add to large pot with water and sea salt. Bring to a boil, stirring for 3 minutes. Turn off fire, skim surface free of foam, and cover for 1 hour. Do not uncover pan!

2. Meantime, chop leeks, celery, and garlic finely. Add boiling water to bouillon cubes, and set aside. Sauté veggies in olive oil until limp, but not browned. Remove from stove and allow to cool. Add to top of blender along with ⅓-cup bouillon and mix thoroughly. Add second ⅓ cup and puree. Transfer to 1-pint container and rinse blender with last ⅓ cup.

3. Add spice mix (C) to B items, and stir to mix. Set aside.

4. After 1 hour, uncover pot and stir. Turn fire back on slow and simmer, covered, for 1 hour, stirring every 15 minutes and crushing undissolved peas against side of pan. Strain slotted spoon through mixture to get any remaining peas. Allow to cool and add to blender and puree. Add back to pot along with vegetable and spice mixture and simmer over low heat. Add water if necessary.

5. Add ham (or Pastrami) about 20 minutes before serving. Add to soup bowls and add some dry sherry at the table.

SZECHUAN SOUP

Ingredients:

A. 2 Cups Chicken Broth
   3 Tbs. Sliced Green Onion Tops
   1½ Tbs. Thinly Sliced Bamboo Shoots
   1½ Tbs. Finely Chopped Reconstituted Wood Ears
   1 Tsp. 5-spice Powder
   1 Tbs. Soy Sauce
   1 Tsp. MSG
   ½ Tsp. Finely Ground Thai Pepper
   ⅛ Tsp. Finely Ground Szechuan Pepper
   ½ Tbs. Brown Sugar
   1 Tsp. Vinegar
   ½ Tsp. Lime Juice

B. 1 Tbs. Rice Flour
   1 Tbs. Water

Directions:

1. Mix all ingredients in "A" and simmer for about 45 minutes. Do not boil.
2. Mix rice flour and water in a cup, then stir into soup and allow to thicken.

VEGETABLE BEEF SOUP

Ingredients:

    1½ Pound Lean Stew Beef
    2 Tbs. Extra Virgin Olive Oil
    2 Cups Leeks, chopped (both green and white parts)
    1½ Cups Mushrooms, chopped
    1½ Cups Potato, peeled and chopped
    1½ Cups Turnips, peeled and chopped
    1 Cup Carrots, peeled and chopped
    1 Cup Celery, chopped
    1 Oz. Pearl Barley
    1 Oz. Small Lima Beans
    1 Oz. Black Beans
    1 Oz. Pink Beans
    1 Oz. Navy Beans
    1 Oz. Small Navy Beans
    ½ Oz. Garbanzos
    ⅓ Oz. Green Split Peas
    ⅓ Oz. Lentils
    1 Clove Garlic, finely chopped
    1 Tbs. Basil
    1 Tbs. Oregano
    1 Tbs. Parsley
    1 Tsp. Thyme
    ½ Tsp. Powdered Rosemary
    Water

Directions:

1. Combine all dried beans in stockpot, cover with water and bring to a boil.
2. Cover; remove from fire and let set for at least 1 hour.
3. Trim beef free from any fat and cut into small cubes. Brown in olive oil, and transfer entire mixture to large stockpot.
4. Add pre-boiled beans and remaining ingredients to beef and simmer, covered for about 2 hours.
5. Serve with a heavy-bodied Merlot.

OTHER SUGGESTIONS

Bouillabaisse
Chilled lentil
Clam Chowder, New England Style
Clam Chowder, New York Style
Cream of Asparagus
Cream of Curried Peas
Cream of Pumpkin
Fish Chowder
French Tarragon
Jambalaya
Philadelphia Pepper Pot
Suimono
Vichyssoise

Chapter 3

I cannot imagine a meal without sauces. They are great on vegetables (*e.g.:* Hollandaise) and on meats (*e.g.:* Bordelaise). This is a critical ingredient when it is time to separate the mundane from the spectacular.

This is a great place for experimentation. Create your own classic sauce. Do not be afraid to use some unconventional ingredients. Try Tamarind, blood oranges, galanga (kha), raisins, spices, etc. Always make sure that it is thick and rich, using a roux or other thickener such as gumbo filé, or even pan drippings.

AVGOLEMONO SAUCE

Ingredients:
>2 Eggs, Whipped in a Bowl
>Juice of 1 Fresh Lemon
>$^1/_2$ Cup Broth (lamb, beef, chicken, or vegetable depending
>>upon the meal; or deglaze the cooking pan for "broth",
>>warmed but not boiling)

Directions:
>Add lemon juice and 1 Tbs. broth to beaten eggs, and continue
to whip. Combine with remaining warm broth in cooking pan and beat
with a small whisk until thickened but not curdled. DO NOT BOIL!
>Pour over Dolmas, Kofte, Vegetables, or use to thicken a soup.

BÉCHAMEL SAUCE

Ingredients:
>1 Large Onion, Finely Chopped
>1 Large Clove Garlic, Chopped
>2 Tbs. Butter
>2 Cups Plain Yogurt

Directions:
>Sauté onion and garlic in butter until limp.
>Stir in yogurt and warm.

BORDELAISE SAUCE

Ingredients:

    A. 2 Tsp. Chopped Shallots
       2 Tbs. Clarified Butter
       ³/₄ Cup Red Wine (Bordeaux!)
    B. 1 Cup Glacé de Viande (or Beef Gravy)
       2 Tbs. Chervil
       ¹/₂ Tsp. Sea Salt
       ¹/₂ Tsp. Cayenne Pepper
       ¹/₄ Tsp. White Pepper
    C. Juice of 1 Lemon
    D. ³/₄ Cup white Bone Marrow poached in white wine

Directions:

1. Cook shallots in clarified butter until limp. Add red wine and reduce to half volume. Add Glacé and spices.
2. Add lemon juice and marrow just prior to serving.
3. This is delicious over steaks, burgers, and other red meat recipes.

CUCUMBER YOGURT SAUCE

Ingredients:

    ¹/₂ Pound Cucumber, peeled, seeded, and chopped
    1 Cup Plain Yogurt
    2 Tsp. Mint
    1 Tsp. Dill
    ¹/₄ Tsp. Coriander
    Pinch Birdseye pepper

Directions:

    Mix all ingredients together and chill for 1 hour before serving.

HOLLANDAISE SAUCE

Ingredients:
>3 Jumbo Egg Yolks
>1 Tbs. Lemon Juice
>$\frac{1}{2}$ Tsp. Sea Salt
>"pinch" of Cayenne Pepper
>1 Stick Unsalted Butter, melted and hot

Directions:
1. Add egg yolks, lemon juice, salt, and pepper to blender. Flick on and off several times
2. Add hot butter slowly while running blender on slow speed.
3. Pour immediately over meal and serve.

MEAT LOAF SAUCE

Ingredients:
>8 Oz. Tomato Paste
>2 Tbs. Salsa
>$1\frac{1}{4}$ Cup Finely Chopped Onions
>1 Tsp. Cumin Powder
>1 Tsp. Cilantro
>$\frac{1}{4}$ Black Pepper
>$\frac{1}{2}$ Tsp. Salt

Directions:
Combine all ingredients in saucepan and cook over low heat for about 15 minutes. Pour over meatloaf before baking.

MINT SAUCE

Ingredients:

1 Quart White Distilled Vinegar (5%)
2 Tbs. Balsamic Vinegar
4 Tbs. Sugar
4 Tbs. Dried Mint, Finely Crushed
10 Black Peppercorns

Directions:

Mix all ingredients and place in airtight bottle. Excellent on lamb, fish and spinach.

MUSHROOM AND CREAM SAUCE

Ingredients:

12 Oz. Oyster Mushrooms, chopped
2 Tbs. Clarified Butter
1 Tsp. Sea Salt
$1/8$ Tsp White Pepper
1 Cup Heavy Cream

Directions:

1. Sauté mushrooms in butter.
2. Add salt and pepper.
3. Add cream and stir until it thickens slightly.
4. Pour over fish.

SEAFOOD COCKTAIL SAUCE

Ingredients:

        1-15 Oz. Can Tomato Sauce
        1 Tsp. Lime Juice
        2 Tsp. Tabasco Sauce (or Habanero Sauce!)
        1 Tbs. Horseradish
        1 Tsp. Caper Liquor
        1 Tsp. Wasabe Powder dissolved in 1 Tbs. Water.
        $\frac{1}{2}$ Tsp. Garlic Powder
        $\frac{1}{2}$ Tsp. Onion Powder
        1 Tsp. Chinese Mustard
        1 Tsp. Ginger, dissolved in 1 Tbs. Water.

Directions:

        Combine all items and simmer for 20 minutes. Add to glass bottle and store in refrigerator.

SOUTHWESTERN CREAM SAUCE

Ingredients:

        1 Tbs. Clarified Butter
        1 Tbs. Flour
        $\frac{1}{2}$ Cup Cream
        1 Tsp. Hungarian Paprika
        $\frac{1}{8}$ Tsp. finely ground HOT pepper, such as Pequin or even Habanero
        $\frac{1}{8}$ Tsp. Cumin Powder
        $\frac{1}{8}$ Tsp. Garlic Powder
        1 Tsp. Cocoa
        1 Tsp. Peanut Butter, diluted with 1 Tbs. Lime Juice

Directions:

1. Make a roux with butter and flour, add cream and other ingredients and stir until slightly thickened.
2. Pour over any seafood dish, or vegetable such as stewed tomatoes, green beans, etc.
3. Serve with any crisp, dry white wine.

SPAGHETTI SAUCE

Ingredients:

      3 Pounds Lean Ground Beef
      2 Medium Onions, Chopped
      2 Bell Peppers, Chopped
      4 Cloves Garlic, Crushed
      2 Cups Chopped Mushrooms
      3 Tbs. Olive Oil
      2-15 Oz. Cans Tomato Sauce
      2-12 Oz. Cans Tomato Paste

Seasonings:

      Add greater amounts, depending on individual tastes.
      1 Tsp. Each—Anchovy Paste
                 Salt
                 Coarse Black Pepper
                 Italian Red Pepper
                 Basil
                 Oregano
    $^1/_2$ Tsp. Each—Celery Leaf
                 Ground Anise or Fennel
                 Powdered Bay Leaf

Directions:

      Brown beef in olive oil. Add onion, bell pepper and garlic. Cook slightly. Add remaining ingredients and simmer, covered, with occasional stirring for three hours or longer, maintaining volume with water.

      Serve over pasta of choice, or use as ingredient in lasagne.

      Appropriate wines: Brunello, Barolo, or Barbaresco.

STOMBOLI SAUCE
(SUGO DI POMODORO ALLA STROMBOLI)

Ingredients:

12 Oz. Still Beer	1 Tsp. Basil
1 Tbs. Lemon Juice	1 Tsp. Sea Salt
$\frac{1}{2}$ Tbs. Brown Sugar	$\frac{1}{2}$ Tsp. Anchovy Paste
6 Oz. Can Tomato Paste	$\frac{1}{2}$ Tsp. Lemon Zest
1 Tsp. Onion Powder	$\frac{1}{4}$ Tsp. Hot Pepper
1 Tsp. Garlic Powder	$\frac{1}{8}$ Tsp. Course Ground Black Pepper

Directions:

Combine all ingredients and simmer until it bubbles like molten lava.

SWEET MARINARA SAUCE

Ingredients:

1-28 Oz. Can of Tomatoes
1 Chopped Medium Onion (1 Cup)
1 Celery Stalk, Chopped ($\frac{1}{3}$ Cup)
3 Tbs. Sweet Bell Pepper, Chopped
1 Tsp. Sugar
$\frac{1}{2}$ Tsp. Sea Salt
$\frac{1}{2}$ Tsp. Basil
$\frac{1}{2}$ Tsp. Oregano
$\frac{1}{2}$ Tsp. Crushed Anise Seed
$\frac{1}{4}$ Tsp. Bay Leaf Powder
3 Tbs. Olive Oil

Directions:

1. Lightly brown veggies in olive oil.
2. Add spices, stir together, then add tomatoes.
3. Simmer, occasionally adding water or white wine to maintain volume.
4. Serve over sweet Italian sausage, ideally on a sub roll, or with fish, poultry or pasta.
5. A semi-sweet white Malvasia, or even Chianti go well with this sauce.

TEXAS BARBECUE SAUCE

Ingredients:

2 Medium Onions
3 Cloves Garlic
1 Cup Pineapple Juice
1$\frac{1}{2}$ Tbs. Lemon Juice
2 Tbs. Cider Vinegar
2 Cubes Beef Bouillon, dissolved in 12 oz. Still Beer
2-15 oz. Cans Tomato Sauce
2 Tbs. each: Dark Brown Sugar, Chili Powder, & Mustard Powder
2 Tbs. Olive Oil
2 Tsp. Cilantro
1 Tsp. Coarse Ground Black Pepper
1 Tsp. Mesquite Powder or Liquid Smoke
1 Tbs. Worcestershire Sauce
$\frac{1}{2}$ Tsp. Hungarian Paprika
$\frac{1}{4}$ Tsp. each: Cayenne Pepper, Habanero Pepper

Optional: $\frac{1}{2}$ Cup of Coffee (A Texan friend of ours does this.)

Directions:

Emulsify onion and garlic in blender with the juices and vinegar. Add to cooking pot, and add remaining ingredients. Cook uncovered, maintaining desired volume with still beer.

YOGURT SAUCE

Ingredients:

$\frac{1}{2}$ Cucumber, peeled, cleaned and chopped
2 Cups Yogurt
1 Tbs. Dried Peppermint, Crumbled
2 Tsp. Dill Weed
$\frac{1}{4}$ Tsp. Hot Red Pepper (e.g.: Birdseye), ground

Directions:

Combine all ingredients and use this user-friendly mix to enhance many meals.

OTHER SUGGESTIONS

Bercy
Beurre Blanc
Beurre Noir
Espagnole
Madeira
Marchands de Vin
Mornay
Mousseline
Perigeaux
Remoulade

Chapter 4

I cannot imagine a salad without a dressing, or many vegetable dishes without any final touch. The basic ingredients are vinegar, oil, and (often) sugar. The vinegar (*e.g.:* Balsamic) lays down the foundation. The oil (extra virgin olive oil, please!), the sugar, herbs and spices make for a characteristic product. Experiment here, as some neat things can be done with such things as capers, anchovy paste, Dijon mustard, etc.

BALSAMIC DRESSING

Ingredients:

1/4 Cup Extra Virgin Olive Oil
2 Tbs. Balsamic Vinegar
1 Tbs. Dijon Mustard
1 Tsp. Sugar
1 Tsp. Caper Liquor

1 Clove Garlic, crushed
1/8 Tsp. Cayenne
1/8 Tsp. White Pepper
1/8 Tsp. Sea Salt.

Directions:

Mix all ingredients in blender and pour over salad.

GUACAMOLE I

Ingredients:

1 Avocado, peeled and diced
1 Tomato, peeled and diced
2 Cloves Garlic, chopped

1/2 Cup Mayonnaise
1 Tbs Cumin
1 Tbs Cilantro

Directions:

Combine all ingredients and mix in a blender.

GUACAMOLE II

Ingredients:

2 Large Avocados, very ripe
1 Onion, chopped finely
2 Cloves Garlic, chopped finely
1 Plum Tomato, cubed
1 Tbs. Chopped Fresh Cilantro
1 Tbs. Lime Juice
1/4 Tsp. Sea Salt

Directions:

Mix ingredients thoroughly and serve with tortilla chips. As
an option, top with refried beans and/or cheese.

GUACAMOLE III

Ingredients:

      2 Ripe Avocados, peeled, seeded and chopped
      1 Ripe Tomato, peeled seeded and chopped
      2 Tbs. Hot Serrano Peppers, seeded and chopped
      $1/2$ Cup Mayonnaise
      2 Tbs. Lime Juice
      1 Tbs. Chopped Onion
      1 Tbs. Fresh Cilantro, chopped (or 1 Tsp. Dried)
      1 Tsp. Chopped Garlic
      $1/4$ Tsp. Sea Salt
      $1/4$ Tsp. Mixed Herb Seasoning

Directions:

1. Combine all ingredients in a blender or food processor until smooth.
2. Refrigerate for at least 30 minutes.
3. Use as a dip, or as a salad, or to top nachos or chalupas.

MARINATED OLIVES

Ingredients:

      $1 1/2$ Cups Select Green Olives, with pits
      1 Cup Italian Dressing
      $1/2$ Tsp. Italian Red Pepper

Directions:

      Cut olives about $1/3$ of the way across the center and roll on cutting board with palm of hand to soften. Add salad dressing and red pepper. Allow at least 4 hours. Excellent by themselves, and delightful when added to Italian Salad.

MIAMI ITALIAN DRESSING

Ingredients:
> $^1/_4$ Cup Vinegar
> 2 Tbs. Lemon Juice
> $^1/_4$ Cup Extra Virgin Olive Oil
> $^1/_8$ Cup Dijon Mustard
> $^1/_4$ Dup Sugar
> $^1/_2$ Tsp. Each: Basil, Oregano, Garlic, Powder, Anchovy Paste
> 1 Tbs. Capers
> 1 Tbs. Juice from Capers
> $^1/_4$ Tsp. Each: Salt, White Pepper

Directions:
> Place all ingredients in blender and run on high speed for 30 seconds. Serve over Italian Salad.

RADICCHIO SALAD

Ingredients:
> 1 Head Radicchio
> 1 cup Boston Lettuce
> $^1/_4$ cup Grated Mozzarella Cheese
> 2 Tbs. Pine Nuts
> 1 Tsp. Capers

Directions:
> Slice Radicchio in half lengthwise, then shred on the diagonal. Shred Boston Lettuce by hand. Add other ingredients and toss. Serve with Balsamic Dressing.

TAPENADE

Ingredients:
- 1¼ Cups Black Olives, drained
- ¾ Cup Tuna (in Oil)
- ½ Cup Dried Figs, dipped in boiling water, stems removed
- ½ Cup Extra Virgin Olive Oil
- ¼ Cup Anchovy Filets
- ¼ Cup Non-pareil Capers
- 1½ Tbs. Lemon Juice
- 1 Tbs. Chinese (Hot) Mustard
- 1 Tbs. Caper Liquor
- ½ Tbs. Chopped Garlic

Directions:
1. Mix all ingredients thoroughly in blender.
2. Serve over toasted French bread (thinly sliced) or crackers or in croustades.
3. A very dry white wine is called for here.

OTHER SUGGESTIONS

Bechamel Sauce
Buttermilk Horseradish Dressing
Fish Veloute
Green Goddess Dressing
Honey Dressing
Milanese
Red Clam
Roquefort or Bleu Cheese
Sour Cream
Thousand Islands
Vinaigrette
White Clam Sauce

Chapter 5

N o meal is complete without at least a small dish of vegetables. I would not like to go on a diet exclusively of veggies, but they do belong. They can be presented in an elegant manner, providing that they are not cooked to death.

My favorites are artichokes, asparagus and beans, through the rest of the alphabet, ending with zucchini.

One does not have to have much in the way of dentition to enjoy these. In fact, I have enjoyed many with my teeth left in the plastic box! Please do not overcook these little darlings!

VEGETABLES

APFELMUS
(Applesauce, Sauce aux Pommes)

Ingredients:
>3 Quarts Apples, peeled, quartered and cored
>2 Cups Water (or better, cider)
>1 Tbs. Refined Sugar
>1 Tbs. Brown Sugar
>1 Tbs. Cinnamon
>1 Tsp. Nutmeg
>1 Tsp. Allspice

OPTIONAL: 2 Tbs. finely chopped Raisins, 2 Tbs. Juice from Pickled Beets, 1/2 Tsp. Ground Cardamom.

Directions:
1. Quarter, core, and peel Apples and add to a covered 6 quart sauce pan along with about 1/2 Tsp. Salt to prevent browning and about 2 quarts water. Drain and rinse before next step.
2. Return rinsed apples to pan, and water or cider and simmer until tender. Mash with potato masher.
3. Add sugar and spices, and cook down to desired thickness. Cover and simmer for an additional hour.
4. Allow to cool to room temperature, or even refrigerate. Serve with smoked sausage, smoked pork chops, sauerbraten, roasted goose, turkey or duckling. A late-picked Riesling (Schloss Johannisberger or Bernkastler Graben are good choices; 1988-1990 are ready).

ASPERAGRASS JEFFERSON*

Ingredients:

1 Pound Fresh Asparagus
  (Small: no larger than $1/2$" dia.!!)
2 Medium Oranges
1 Tbs. Grenadine Syrup
1 Medium Lemon

3 Egg Yolks
1 Tbs. Grand Marnier
12 Tbs. Butter (melted
  and still very hot)
$1/4$ Tsp. White Pepper

Directions:

1. Steam Asparagus to "al dente" doneness, set aside and keep warm.
2. Add zest from 1 orange and 1 lemon, juice from 2 oranges and Grenadine** to small sauce pan and reduce volume to $1/4$ cup.
3. Add egg yolks and juice from $1/2$ lemon (2 Tbs.) to a blender along with pepper and Grand Marnier. Add cooked-down Zest mixture and mix lightly.
4. Turn the blender to "high" and slowly add hot butter. Mix until thick. Arrange asparagus on plate and top with sauce.

*Thomas Jefferson introduced "Asperagrass" to Virginia following one of his many visits to Europe.

**If you can find them, 2 Blood Oranges are preferable to the use of Grenadine.

BOSTON BAKED BEANS

Ingredients:

1 Pound Canned White Beans
$1/4$ Pound Smoked Sausage or
  Frankfurters, sliced $1/4$" thick
2 Tbs. Molasses
1 Tbs. Brown Sugar

1 Tbs. Prepared Mustard
1 Tbs. Catsup
1 Tsp. Sea Salt
$1/8$ Tsp. of a mix of red,
  white and black peppers

Directions:

1. Combine all ingredients, ideally in a clay pot, and bake at 375° F. for about 20 minutes.
2. Serve with Brown Bread.

CABBAGE ROLLS

Ingredients:

      1½ Pounds Ground Beef (80% lean)
      ¾ Pound Ground Pork (80% lean)
      1 Medium Onion, finely chopped
      1 Clove Garlic, finely chopped
      1¼ Cups Uncooked Rice
      12-Oz. Can Tomato Paste
      1 Tbs. Cinnamon
      1 Tbs. Ground Sage
      2 Tsp. Sea Salt
      2 Tsp. Pepper

      1 Large Head Cabbage, parboiled and leaves removed

Directions:

Combine all ingredients and roll in pre-cooked cabbage leaves. Freeze all rolls not planned for immediate use. Place rest in steamer and cook for at least 3 hours, adding water when necessary. Serve with a tomato sauce such as the following.

TOMATO SAUCE

Ingredients:

      1 Small Onion, finely chopped
      1 Clove Garlic, finely chopped
      3 Tbs. Clarified Butter
      2 Tbs. Flour
      1-16 Oz. Can Tomato Sauce

Directions:

Sauté onion and garlic in clarified butter, remove from pan. Add remaining butter and flour to make a roux. Stir in tomato sauce and thicken. Re-add onion and garlic, stir. Pour over steamed cabbage rolls.

Serve with a light bodied, semi-sweet red wine such as a Polish red currant wine, or a Lambrusco, or Kir.

CHALUPAS SAN ANTONIO

Ingredients:

A. 1 Green Bell Pepper, seeded and chopped
1 Yellow Onion, Chopped
3 Cloves Garlic, Chopped

B. 8 Oz. Can of Tomato Paste
2-4 Tbs. Hot Picante Sauce, ideally: Salsa Mansa
2 Tbs. Chili Powder
1 Tbs. Cumin Powder
$\frac{1}{2}$ Tsp. Salt
$\frac{1}{2}$ Tsp. Cilantro Powder
$\frac{1}{4}$ Tsp. Black Pepper

C. 12 Corn Tortillas
4 Tbs. Corn Oil
3 Tbs. Butter

D. 6 Jumbo Eggs, fried in butter

E. 1 Pound Goat Cheese, grated (Monterrey Jack will do)

F. 15 Oz. Can of Garbanzos
Fresh Cilantro Leaves

Directions:

1. Brown items in "A" in corn oil. Reserve a portion, uncooked, for garnish.
2. Mix sauce in "B" and add to pan with "A". Simmer.
3. Gently and quickly soften tortillas in oil and butter. Place in "hold warm" oven.
4. Fry eggs in butter.
5. Warm Garbanzos in pan.
6. Place a layer of garbanzos on a plate, top with a tortilla, the sauce and a sprinkling of cheese.
7. Add a 2nd tortilla and top with more sauce, cheese, and an egg.
8. Garnish with raw onion, green pepper and cilantro.
9. Serve with a quality Mexican beer, such as Bohemia.

CRANBERRY WINE DELIGHT

Ingredients:

> 3 Cups Fresh Cranberries
> 1½ Cups Sugar
> Zest of 1 Orange
> 1¼ Cups Red Port Wine
> 1½ Tbs. Corn Starch

Directions:

1. Mix first 4 ingredients and heat to a light boil. Reduce heat, cover and simmer for 5 minutes until berries pop.
2. Separately, mix ¼ cup of cold water with cornstarch and add to mixture, stirring until thickened.
3. Chill for several hours before serving.

EGGPLANT CAVIAR
(After the Traditional Ukrainian Dish)

Ingredients:

> A. 1 Eggplant, boiled for 25 minutes, stemmed and peeled, chopped finely (~18 oz.)
> 2 Medium Onions (~12 oz.) peeled and chopped
> 6 oz. Can Tomato Paste
> 1 Tsp. Chopped Garlic
> ½ Tsp. Sea Salt
> ½ Tsp. Anchovy Paste or Fish Sauce
> ½ Tsp. Brown Sugar
> B. Extra Virgin Olive Oil
> C. ½ Tsp. Lemon Juice per serving

Directions:

1. Sauté onion in 2 Tbs. olive oil until limp.
2. Add Eggplant and garlic and stir until soft. Add more olive oil if necessary.
3. Add remaining ingredients and stir until done.
4. Chill and serve cold with any meat dish. Add lemon juice just before serving. A good Merlot sings with this!

FRIED EGGPLANT CURRY

Ingredients:
    1 Eggplant, peeled and cut into ½" spears
    1 Tsp. Madras 14 Spice Powder
    1 Tsp. Turmeric
    Bread Crumbs
    Whipped Eggs
    Vegetable and Sesame Oil, Mixed to Taste

Directions:
1. Heat Oils in Pan.
2. Add Spices to Whipped Eggs.
3. Dip Eggplant spears in eggs and coat thoroughly.
4. Roll spears in Bread Crumbs and fry until golden colored.
5. Serve with Cucumber Yogurt Sauce.

FRIED RICE

Ingredients:
A. 2 Cups Cooked Rice
B. 2 Tbs. Carrots, Finely Chopped
    2 Tbs. Celery, Finely Chopped
    1½ Tsp. Ginger, Finely Chopped
C. ¼ Cup Cooked Leftover Meat, Chopped
    ¼ Cup Bok Choy Greens, Finely Chopped
    2 Tbs. Shiitake Mushrooms, Finely Chopped
    2 Tbs. Wood Ears, Finely Chopped
    ½ Tsp. MSG
    ¼ Tsp. Szechuan Pepper (freshly ground)
D. Oil: 1 Tbs. Sesame Oil, 1 Tbs. Peanut Oil
    Soy Sauce: 1½ Tbs.

Directions:
1. Prepare rice, ideally use Jasmine rice.
2. Add to wok (or large skillet) oil mixture and heat for 1-2 minutes. Add ingredients in "B" plus soy sauce. Stir-fry for 1 minute, then mix in rice. Stir-fry for 5 minutes.
3. Add in ingredients from "C" and stir-fry for another 5 minutes.
4. Serve with a white wine to which has been added some pickled ginger (Shoga).

FRITTATA

Ingredients:

    1 Cup Zucchini, shredded
    $^1/_2$ Cup Carrots, peeled and shredded
    $^3/_4$ Cup Ham, finely diced, or use Hot Italian Sausage
        (cooked & drained), or omit altogether for a vegetarian
        dish, adding additional zucchini.
    2 Roma Tomatoes, peeled and thinly sliced
    8 Eggs, slightly beaten
    $^1/_4$ Cup Light Cream
    2 Cloves Garlic, chopped
    1 Tbs. Flour
    $^1/_4$ Cup Romano Cheese
    $^1/_2$ Tsp. Each: Basil, Oregano, Red Pepper, Cilantro, Sea Salt
    $^1/_4$ Tsp. white Pepper
    3 Tbs. Extra Virgin Olive Oil
    Clarified Butter
    Plain Bread Crumbs
    Hungarian Paprika

Directions:

1. Sauté ham in 1 Tbs. olive oil and set aside.
2. Sauté zucchini and carrots in 2 Tbs. olive oil until limp, but not browned. Drain and set aside.
3. Lightly beat eggs, and then add cream, flour and Romano cheese. Beat until mixed thoroughly.
4. Line a 10" quiche dish with butter, then breadcrumbs, and dust with Hungarian Paprika.
5. Add salt, pepper, spices and meat to egg mixture.
6. Place sautéed vegetables on bottom of quiche dish, cover with tomato slices, then pour egg mixture over top.
7. Bake for 25 minutes at 375 deg. F until done.
8. Invert on plate and serve.
9. Any light, dry to semi-sweet wine is appropriate here.

HOMINY FOUNTAINHEAD

Ingredients:
>1 Pound Can Hominy, drained & rinsed
>$^1/_2$ Stick of Butter
>$^1/_4$ Cup Chopped Bell Pepper
>$1^1/_2$ Tbs. Shallots (or Green Onions), chopped
>1 Tsp. Chopped Garlic
>$^1/_8$ Tsp. Cayenne Pepper
>$^1/_8$ Tsp. White Pepper
>$^1/_8$ Tsp. Black Pepper
>2 Tbs. Lime Juice
>$^1/_4$ Cup Still Beer
>$^1/_4$ Cup Chopped Smithfield Ham

Directions:
1. Fry bell pepper, shallots and garlic in 2 Tbs. melted butter.
2. Add hominy, remaining butter and remaining ingredients. Stir until partially thickened and serve.

KARTOFFELKUCHEN

Ingredients:
>3 Medium Potatoes, scrubbed thoroughly, but not peeled
>2 Eggs, Beaten
>Flour
>Clarified Butter
>Pepper Mix (equal parts Cayenne, Black and White place in a shaker)

Directions:
1. Scrape potatoes on a course grater and dredge with flour. Add to beaten eggs and mix.
2. Separate into 6 equal pieces and form each piece into a pattie about $^3/_4$" thick. Sprinkle on both sides with pepper mix.
3. Fry over low heat in clarified butter until browned on both sides.

KARTOFFELSALAT
(German Potato Salad)

Ingredients:

2 Medium Potatoes, scrubbed and cut into 8-10 pieces
6 Slices of Bacon, Fried (reserve grease)
$^1/_4$ Cup Beef Bouillon
1 Tsp. Marjoram
$^1/_2$ Tsp. Dill Weed
$^1/_4$ Tsp. Mace
$^1/_8$ Tsp. White Pepper
$^1/_8$ Tsp. Black Pepper
2 Tbs. Vinegar, ideally Herbal

Directions:

1. Lightly boil potatoes and peel while still warm.
2. Crush bacon and set aside.
3. Dust potatoes with herbs and add bouillon.
4. Add mix of vinegar and $^1/_4$ cup bacon grease.
5. Mix thoroughly and allow to set at room temperature for at least 2 hours before serving. Do not refrigerate!

PEARL BARLEY PILAF

Ingredients:

12 Ounces Pearl Barley soaked in water for 4 hours
$^1/_4$ cup chopped shallots
1 cup chopped mushrooms
1 cup Chicken Bouillon
1 tsp. powdered bay leaf
1 tsp. Ginger
1 tsp. thyme
1 tbs. turmeric
Extra Virgin Olive Oil

Directions:

1. Sauté shallots and mushrooms in olive oil.
2. Combine with remaining ingredients. Mix thoroughly and refrigerate for two hours prior to serving.
3. Goes well with fish or chicken recipes, and a good bottle of Gewürztraminer

TASSOS POTATOES

Ingredients:
    A. 2 Medium Baked Potatoes

    B. 1 Cup Cooked Ham, cut into small ($1/4$") cubes.
      $1/2$ Tsp. Each:
          Garlic Powder
          Red Pepper (cayenne or Tabasco)
          Black Pepper
          White Pepper
      2 Tbs. Clarified Butter, Melted

    C. 1 Cup Grated Cheese: $3/4$ Cup Sharp Cheddar, $1/4$ Cup Swiss

    D. $1/4$ Cup Sour Cream
      2 Tsp. Chives
      Hungarian Paprika

Directions:
1. Make Tassos as follow: Mix garlic and the 3 peppers in a bowl. Roll the ham pieces in the mix until coated. Fry briefly in clarified butter.
2. Slice baked potatoes lengthwise, carefully spoon out contents, mash, and then mix with Tassos and place mixture back in skins.
3. Top with cheese and return to oven. Bake for 15 minutes, or until cheese melts.
4. Top with sour cream and chives.

OTHER SUGGESTIONS

Acorn squash with maple syrup
Baked stuffed eggplant
Baked tomatoes with tapenade
Broccoli in Hollandaise
Cassoulet
Curried Chick Peas
Eggplant Parmesan
French Style Green Beans
Harvard Beets
Polenta and Sausage
Ratatouille Niçoise
Steak Oscar
Stuffed Green Peppers
Zucchini alla Marinara

Chapter 6

Throughout history baked goods have been a staple of good nutrition. They are rich in complex carbohydrates, and offer a significant amount of protein. Numerous grains have been used to make these products. Experiment here.

Baked goods can include meat and fish dishes. A good quiche, a frittata and the savory soufflés and fondues are grand testament to just how wonderful they can be.

There is a great deal of information available in numerous cookbooks elsewhere. This section is limited to only those originating in our kitchen. Several great ideas from the "other folks" are listed at the end of this chapter.

BOSTON BROWN BREAD

Ingredients:

2 Cups Graham Flour
1 Cup all-purpose Flour
2 Cups Buttermilk
$1/2$ Cup Brown Sugar
$1/2$ Cup Molasses
2 Tsp. Baking Soda
1 Tsp. Sea Salt
1 Jumbo Egg, Whipped
1 Tbs. Melted Clarified Butter
$1/2$ Cup Raisins

Directions:

1. Combine all ingredients and pour into "tin cans". Bake at 325° F. for as long as it takes for a toothpick to come out clean.
2. Remove the bottoms of the tin cans and push out Brown Bread.
3. Slice about $3/4$ inch thick and serve with sweet cream butter, and possibly honey. An alternative is whipped cream.

FETTUCCINI ALFREDO

Ingredients:

1 Pound Fettuccini or Linguini
2 Qts. Boiling Water
2 Tbs. Olive Oil
$1^1/2$ Cups Clarified Butter
$3/4$ Cup Heavy Cream
2 Cups Romano Cheese
$1/2$ Tsp. White Pepper

Directions:

1. Add salt, oil and pasta to boiling water and cook until "al dente".
2. Drain and add to pan with melted clarified butter; add cream.
3. Gradually stir in Romano Cheese and white pepper.

FRENCH TOAST

Ingredients:

8 slices White Bread, Crusts removed

2 Eggs, whipped to a foam, but not stiff

$\frac{1}{2}$ Tsp. Sea Salt

$\frac{1}{4}$ Tsp. Nutmeg, Cinnamon, and Vanilla Extract

1 Tsp. Brown Sugar

1 Stick Butter

$\frac{1}{2}$ Pint Maple Syrup (only the real thing!)

Directions:

1. Dip both sides of bread in egg and even coating with a table knife.
2. Place on a well-buttered griddle and lightly brown, flip over and lightly brown other side. Place in serving dish and hold in a warm oven until all slices are done.
3. Butter 1 slice and add syrup, top with a second slice and butter and cover with syrup.

HUMMUS

Ingredients:

15 Oz. Can of Chick Peas, drained and hulls removed

1 Tsp. Tabasco Sauce (or better: Chili Oil!)

1 Tbs. Olive Oil

1 Tbs. Lemon Juice

1 Tsp. Cumin

1 Tsp. Garlic Powder

$\frac{1}{2}$ Tsp. Dill Weed

Directions:

1. Cover Chick Peas (Garbanzos, Ceci) with water in a saucepan and simmer until tender. Mash with a potato masher, and stir in remaining ingredients. Simmer until thick.
2. Serve in Pita Quarters with some Cucumber Yogurt.

PIE CRUST

Ingredients:

2 Cups Flour
1 Stick Unsalted Butter, placed in freezer then cut into 6 pieces
$^1/_3$ Cup Cold Water

Directions:

1. Put flour and butter in food processor. Blend until in pea-sized pieces (30-45 seconds).
2. Add cold water and blend until dough becomes a large ball.
3. Divide in half and roll out halves on a floured board. Place in a well-buttered pie pan and add mixture of whatever you wish to bake. Top with other half, or a lattice, or leave open, depending on the meal.

QUICHE ALSACE

Ingredients:

2$^1/_2$ Cups Shredded Swiss Cheese
  (Better: Lorraine Cheese)
12 Slices Crisp Bacon, Chopped
1 Shallot, Chopped
2 Cloves Garlic, Crushed
$^1/_4$ Cup Red Onion, Chopped
5 Jumbo Eggs
2 Cups Heavy Cream
$^3/_4$ Tsp. Sea Salt

$^1/_2$ Tsp. Ea.: Black Pepper,
  White Pepper,
  Cayenne Pepper,
  Nutmeg, Ginger
Clarified Butter
Pie Crust for 9" Pan
Grated Romano Cheese
Hungarian Paprika

Directions:

1. Place piecrust in well-buttered 9-10" quiche dish. Top with cheese, garlic, shallot, onion and bacon.
2. Beat eggs and cream until thick, adding spices to mixture. Pour over other ingredients in quiche dish. Dust with Romano cheese and paprika.
3. Bake at 375° F for 45 minutes, or until firm (test with toothpick inserted 1" from outside edge).
4. Serve with an Alsatian Gewürztraminer.

RUM CAKE

Ingredients:

1-2 Liters of Dark Rum
2½ Cups All Purpose Flour
1 Cup Light Brown sugar
1 Cup Unsalted Butter
1 Cup Buttermilk
½ Cup Chopped Black Walnuts

½ Cup Dried Fruit
2 Large Eggs, whipped in a
bowl
2 Tsp. Baking Powder
1 Tsp. Baking Soda
1 Tsp. Lemon Extract

Directions:

Before you start, sample the rum to check for quality. Good isn't it? Now go ahead. Select a large mixing bowl, measuring cup, etc. Check the rum again. It must be just right. To be sure rum is of the highest quality, pour 1 level cup of rum into a glass and drink it as fast as you can. Repeat . . . With an electric mixer, beat 1 cup of butter in a large fluffy bowl. Add 1 seaspoon of thugar and beat again.

Meanwhile, make sure that the rum is of the finest quality. Try another cup. Open second liter if necessary. Add 2 arge leggs, 2 cups fried druit and beat until high. If druit gets stuck in beaters, must pry it loose with a drewscriver. Sample the rum again, checking for tonscisticity. Next sift 3 cups of pepper or salt (it really doesn't matter). Sample the rum again. Sift ½ pint of lemon juice. Fold in chopped butter and your strained nuts. Add 1 babblespoon of brown thugar, or whatever color you can find. Wix mel. Grease oven and turn cake pan to 350 gredees. Now, pour the whole mess into the coven . . . and brake. Check the rum again, and bo to ged.

SOPAIPILLAS

Ingredients:

4 Cups Flour
½ Cup Warm Water
1 Tsp. Sugar, 1 Tsp. Sea Salt
1 Package Dry Yeast
("proofed" with water & sugar)
1 Tbs. Soft Butter

1 Egg, plus 1 Eggyolk
½ Tsp. Ginger
¼ Tsp. Vanilla
½ Tsp. Nutmeg, or Tamarind
Hot Corn Oil for Frying

Directions:

Mix ingredients and let rise to double. Roll ¼" thick and cut into pieces about 1" x 2". Fry until browned in hot oil. Serve with local honey.

SOUFFLE FOUNTAINHEAD

Ingredients:

> 5 Jumbo Eggs, separated and kept covered at room temperature
> for 1 hour
> 1 Cup Cheddar Cheese, grated (ideally white cheddar)
> 1 Cup Chopped Ham
> 3 Tbs. Butter
> 3 Tbs. Flour
> 1 Cup Milk
> 1 Tsp. Parsley
> 1 Tsp. Chervil
> 1 Tsp. Thyme
> $1/2$ Tsp. Powdered Bay Leaf
> $1/4$ Tsp. Black Pepper
> $1/4$ Tsp. White Pepper
> Plain Bread Crumbs
> Butter

Directions:

1, Melt butter in saucepan, add flour, and make a roux. Add milk and cook about 5 minutes, remove from fire and then slowly add whipped egg yolks.
2. Add shallots, ham, cheese and spices. Cook about 3 minutes.
3. Whip egg whites until stiff.
4. Mix $1/3$ of egg whites to yolk mixture gently. Add to soufflé dish which has been coated with butter and breadcrumbs. Then gently fold in remaining egg whites. Bake for 20-25 minutes at 375° F.
5. Serve with a Gewürztraminer, a Vidal, or a Malvasia.

OTHER SUGGESTIONS

Challah Braided Bread
Challah with Dark Rye and Raisins
Chapati
Croissants
French Bread
Italian Bread

Naan Bread
Pita Bread
Pumpernickel Bread
Sourdough Bread
Wheat-Germ Bread

Chapter

Younger cuts of meat such as veal and lamb are user friendly for the "dentally impaired". This is especially so when they are finely chopped or ground. Pain de Veau and Moussaka come to mind here. Pork (especially when "certified") and beef can be also delightful. The tenderloin cuts of each can be particularly good. Insist on the top of the line on beef. An upper "choice" from Angus or Hereford cooked rare with spices and sauces is a great way to go.

The list herein covers the four types of meats, and in their most easily eaten forms.

MEATS

KALBSBURGER

Ingredients:

> 1 Pound Ground Veal
> 1 Tbs. Chopped Shallots
> 1 Tsp. Ginger
> ½ Tsp. Each: Sea Salt, White Pepper, Mustard, and Tarragon

Directions:

Mix and allow to equilibrate for 1 hour. Form into 4 oval patties and cook on grill with olive oil until rare. Serve on Bavarian Black Bread or Dark Pumpernickel. Serve with a dry high-quality wine such as a Steinberger Spatlese.

KONIGSBERGER KLOPSE*

Ingredients:

> A. ½ Pound Lean Ground Pork
>   ½ Pound Ground Veal
>   3-4 Chopped Shallots
>   2 Chopped Garlic Cloves
>   1 Cup Plain Bread Crumbs
>   ½ Tbs. Dried Parsley
>   ½ Tbs. Dried Chervil
>   2 Tsp. Salt
>   1 Tsp. Black Pepper
>   3 Eggs, lightly beaten
>   together with 1 Tbs.
>   Anchovy Paste
>
> B. 2 cups Beef Broth
>   1 Tbs Gravy Sauce (eg. Kitchen Bouquet)
>   1 C. White Wine (Riesling or Gewürztramminer)
>
> C. 3 Egg Yolks
>   2 Tbs. Cornstarch
>   2 Tbs. White Wine
>   1 Cup Yogurt

Directions:

Combine ingredients in A, and set aside for 30 minutes (refrigerated) to allow bread crumbs to de-glutinate. Mix ingredients in B in deep skillet and bring to a slow boil while rolling the mixture from Part A into about 24 small meatballs (actually more like dumplings!). Simmer the meatballs in mixture B for 20 minutes. Meanwhile, whip together ingredients in C with a small whisk. Remove meatballs and add mixture C to pan, stirring with whisk until thickened. Add back meatballs and stir for about 3 minutes.

Serve with a 4-star German wine—a Kabinett or Spatlese. Personal choices: Schloss Johannisberger, 1989; Steinberger, 1990.

* This classic East Prussian dish has been prepared for over 600 years under various names—Klops, Closse, Knodel, Kotbulla, among them. Even Konigsberg has its variants: Koenigsberg, and presently Kaliningrad under its current Russian Rule).

MATSU BALLS
(Calf Fries)

NOTE: This is NOT to be confused with Knaidlach (Matzo Balls)*

Legend has it that this recipe originated in Esashi, Japan, on the Island of Hokkaido. Interestingly, the local population is the Ainu, a Caucasian group.

The local cattle are a feral breed, derived from the Matsushita strain, it is said. The bulls are apparently somewhat aggressive. It is apparently for this reason that during the spring equinox that the hunters are sent to convert the bull calves into steers. The leftover part is a formidable delicacy, which is not easily obtained in the United States.**

This is a recipe that considers the original concept, but is done otherwise.

Ingredients:
>   1 Pound Ground Veal, 80% Lean
>   1 Jumbo Egg, Whipped
> $^1/_2$ Tsp. Garlic Powder
>   1 Tsp. Sea Salt
> $^1/_2$ Cup Plain Bread Crumbs
> $^1/_4$ Tsp. Mace

Sauce:
> $^1/_4$ Pound Unsalted Butter
>   2 Tbs. Lemon Juice
> $^1/_2$ Tsp. Tabasco Sauce

Directions:
1. Mix all ingredients and allow to stand for 30 minutes.
2. Form into appropriate shape.
3. Simmer in a 50:50 mix of olive oil and clarified butter until lightly browned, turning frequently.
4. Serve with sauce and a good dry white wine. Gewürztraminer is a great choice.

*This is NOT Kosher for Passover! Beef + Dairy + Breadcrumbs are a major NO-NO!

**All of the above is a total fabrication. If you believed it, I have a nice swamp front lot to sell you in Florida!

MUNSON FARM MORELS AND VEAL

Ingredients:

A. 1 Pound Ground Milk Fed Veal
   $^1/_4$ Cup Chopped Onions
   $^1/_4$ Cup Bread Crumbs + 1 Tbs. Soy Flour
   2 Tsp. Parsley
   $^1/_2$ Tsp. Sea Salt
   $^1/_2$ Tsp. White Pepper
   $^1/_4$ Tsp. Dill Weed
   $^1/_4$ Tsp. Powdered Bay Leaf
   $^1/_4$ Tsp. Cardamom
   2 Eggs, Whipped in a Cup

B. 1 Tbs. Corn Oil
   1 Tbs. Soy Bean Oil

C. $10^1/_2$ Ounce Can Beef Broth (Better: Glacé de Viande)
   12 Morel Mushrooms, Slightly Chopped ($^3/_4$ Cup)
   1 Tbs. Cornstarch
   1 Tbs. Butter

Directions:

1. Combine all ingredients in A and make into 4 patties. Fry lightly in oil mixture. Do not over cook.
2. Make a roux of butter and cornstarch, stirring until blended and thickened. Add beef broth and stir until slightly thickened. Add morels at end, stir for 2 minutes, and pour over patties.
3. Serve with Carlsberg beer or Tuborg.
4. Great side dishes are creamed corn and herbal bread.

PAIN DE VEAU

Ingredients:

2# Ground Veal
3 Tbs. chopped Shallots
1½ Tsp. Garlic
8 Button mushrooms, chopped
3 morels, chopped
½ Cup plain bread crumbs

2 Large Eggs
1 Tsp. each: Tarragon, Sea Salt
½ Tsp. Anise Powder, Cayenne,
  and White Pepper
1 Tbs. Lemon juice.

Directions:

1. Brown garlic, shallots, then mushrooms in clarified butter.
2. Add to veal, along with eggs, breadcrumbs and spices. Combine.
3. Place in well-buttered bread pan and bake at 350° F. for 45 minutes. Brush top with melted butter before placing in oven.
4. Serve with a good Chardonnay or a dry White Bordeaux.

VEAL MEATBALLS MARINARA

Ingredients:

1 Pounds Ground Veal
¼ Cup Romano Cheese
¼ Cup Plain Bread Crumbs
2 Tbs. Dried Parsley
1 Tsp. Oregano
1 Tsp. Basil
1 Tsp. Sea Salt
½ Tsp. Course Ground Black Pepper

Marinara Sauce (See Index)
Linguini
Extra Virgin Olive Oil
Romano Cheese for Garnish

Directions:

1. Combine Veal with next 7 ingredients. Let rest for 30 minutes. Then roll into walnut-sized balls.
2. Brown meatballs in olive oil.
3. Add to Marinara Sauce and simmer until done.
4. Serve over linguini and top with Romano Cheese.
5. This meal is wonderful when served with garlic bread and an Italian vegetable.
6. Any of the three "B's" of Italian wines is most appropriate. Our choice would be Brunello.

VEAL PATTIES MARSALA

Ingredients:

    A. 1 Pound Ground Veal, pressed into 6 thin patties
         1 Tbs. Butter
         1 Tbs. Extra Virgin Olive Oil
         2 Tbs. Flour
         Salt & Pepper to taste

    B. $1/2$ Cup Beef Stock
         $1/3$ Cup Morels
         $1/2$ Tsp. Dried Parsley
         $1/2$ Tsp. Dried Oregano
         $1/8$ Tsp. Powdered Bay Leaf

    C. $1/2$ Cup Marsala Wine

Directions:

1. Lightly coat veal patties with flour and cook briefly in butter and oil mixture. Remove patties and store in warm oven.
2. De-glaze pan with beef stock, add spices and simmer.
3. Add Marsala and patties and simmer for 2 minutes.
4. Serve over pasta or rice.

KIBBEH

Ingredients:

       1½ Pounds Ground Lamb

       2 Medium Onions, Chopped

       2 Cloves Garlic, Minced

       1¼ Cups Bulgar Wheat

       ¼ Cup Olive Oil

       1 Cup Water

       ½ Tsp. Salt

       ¼ Tsp. Course Black Pepper

       Butter or Margarine

Seasoning Mixture:

       ½ Cup Pine Nuts, Chopped

       1 Tsp. Salt

       ½ Tsp. Course Ground Black Pepper

       1 Tbs. Mint

       2 Tbs. Parsley

       1½ Tsp. Cinnamon

       1 Tsp. Dill Weed

Directions:

Combine Bulgar Wheat, 1 cup water, and ¼ cup olive oil and set aside at room temperature for 1 hour. Add salt, pepper, and 1 chopped onion. Fold in ½ pound of ground lamb. (Comment: often the entire 1½ pounds are added, and the mixture is served raw, as is).

Combine 1 pound of ground lamb, 1 onion, garlic, and seasoning mixture.

Place ½ of Bulgar mixture in well-buttered baking dish, cover with the lamb mixture, then top with the rest of the Bulgar mixture. Sprinkle top with 1 Tsp. of dill weed. Bake at 350° F. for 45 minutes. Makes 8 servings.

Serve with a good Cabernet Sauvignon.

KOFTE

Ingredients:

3/4 Pound Lean Ground Lamb
1/2 Cup Plain Bread Crumbs
1 Finely Chopped Medium Onion
1 Clove Garlic, Finely Chopped
1 Tsp. Sea Salt
1 Tsp. Cumin Powder
1/2 Tsp. Cayenne Pepper

1/2 Tsp. White Pepper
1/2 Tsp. Black Pepper
1/2 Tsp. Thyme
1/2 Tsp. Mint
1/2 Tsp. Cinnamon
1/4 Tsp. Dill Weed

Directions:

Mix all ingredients thoroughly. Either stuff meat mixture into sausage casings or form into walnut-sized balls. Brown in olive oil, then simmer covered after adding water, for 10 minutes. Serve with Pita Bread with lettuce, tomato slices, and cucumber/yogurt sauce.

Serve with a dry red wine, such as Demestica.

MOUSSAKA

Ingredients

2 Large Eggplants, Peeled &
    Sliced About 1/4 in. Thick
1 1/4 Pounds Ground Lamb
28 oz. Can Plum Tomatoes
1 Small Can Tomato Paste
1 Medium Onion, Chopped
2 Cloves Garlic, Crushed

2 Tsp. Ground, Dried Peppermint
1 Tsp. Ground Cinnamon
1 Tsp. Black Pepper
1 Cup Burgundy
3 Cups Béchamel Sauce
Parmesan Cheese
Olive Oil

Directions:

Sauté onion and garlic in olive oil, add lamb and brown. Add tomatoes, tomato paste, wine and seasonings. Simmer for 2 hours, covered.

Fry eggplant slices in olive oil until lightly browned and limp. Line the bottom and sides of baking dish with eggplant slices, then top with meat mixture. Top with Béchamel Sauce and sprinkle with Parmesan (or Romano, if available).

Bake at 375 degrees for 15 to 20 minutes, or until slightly browned.

Serve with a heavy-bodied red wine such as a Brunello or Chateauneuf-du-Pape.

GREAT BALLS OF FIRE!

Ingredients:
>1½ Pounds Lean Ground Beef
>1½ Pounds Lean Ground Pork
>2 Tbs. Dried Parsley
>¾ Cup Plain Bread Crumbs
>4 Eggs, Whipped in a bowl
>¼ Cup Romano Cheese
>1 Tbs. Basil
>1 Tbs. Oregano
>½ Tsp. White Pepper
>1 Tbs. Italian Red Pepper, Finely Ground
>½ Tsp. Habanero Pepper, Finely Ground
>¼ Tsp. Birdseye Pepper, Finely Ground
>Extra Virgin Olive Oil
>Pesto Genovese
>Marinara Sauce (See Index)

Directions:
1. Combine ingredients, beef through peppers. Mix and roll into walnut-sized balls. Brown in Olive Oil.
2. Serve with Marinara Sauce, Linguini with Pesto sauce, Garlic Bread, Miami Salad (see Index), and of course, Chianti.

HAM SALAD

Ingredients:
>1½ Cups Chopped Cooked Ham
>½ Cup Pickle Relish
>½ Cup Mayonnaise
>1 Tbs. Non-Pareil Capers
>½ Tsp. Garlic Powder
>½ Tsp. Black Pepper
>½ Tsp. Hungarian Paprika
>Light Rye Bread

Directions:
1. Mix ingredients thoroughly and place in refrigerator.
2. Spread on rye bread and serve with a quality Riesling.

HUNAN MEATBALLS

Ingredients:

 1 Pound Lean Ground Beef
 ½ Pound Lean Ground Pork
 1½ Tbs. Fresh Ginger, chopped or minced
 1 Tbs. Rice Flour
 ¼ Tsp. Ground Thai Pepper
 ¼ Tsp. 5 spice powder
 ¼ Tsp. Sea Salt
 ¼ Tsp. MSG
 ½ Cup Peanut Oil
 1 Tbs. Sesame Oil

Finishing Sauce:

 1 Tbs. Corn Starch
 ½ Cup Chicken Broth
 2 Tbs. Soy Sauce
 1½ Tbs. Brown Sugar
 ¼ Tsp. Sea Salt

Directions:

1. Combine first 8 items in "A", and roll into 24 meatballs. Brown in oil mixture.
2. Mix cornstarch in a small amount of chicken broth and make into a paste. Add remaining ingredients and simmer until slightly thickened. Pour over meatballs.
3. Serve with a Tsingtao Beer.

MEAT AND CHEESE LOAF

Ingredients:

1 Pound Lean Ground Beef
1 Pound Lean Ground Pork
2 Eggs, whipped in Bowl
1 Cup Chopped Onion
2 Cloves Garlic, Crushed
$1/4$ Cup Chopped Peppers, Bell or Hot Hungarian
$1/2$ Cup Plain Bread Crumbs
1 Tsp. Parsley
1 Tsp. Oregano
$1/2$ Tsp. Sea Salt
$1/4$ Tsp. Black Pepper
1 Cup Shredded Sharp Cheddar Cheese

Directions:

Combine first 3 ingredients in a mixing bowl, and add all remaining ingredients except cheese. Allow to rest for 15 minutes. Spread out on waxed paper to make a rectangle about 12"x18", and cover surface with cheese. Use waxed paper to help roll into a tight loaf. Place in baking dish and top with Meat Loaf Sauce (see Index).

Bake at 350° F. for about 45 minutes to 1 hour, or until done to desired degree.

MEATBALLS MARINARA

Ingredients:

2 Pounds Ground Veal
$1^1/2$ Pounds Ground Pork
$1/2$ Cup Plain Bread Crumbs
1 Egg, Whipped in a Cup
$1/4$ Cup Cream
2 Tsp. Basil
1 Tsp. Bay Leaf Powder

2 Tsp. Oregano
1 Tsp. Thyme
$1/2$ Tsp. White Pepper
2 Tsp. Hot Italian Pepper
2 Tbs. Capers
$1/4$ Cup Romano Cheese

Directions:

1. Mix all ingredients together and roll into walnut sized balls.
2. Brown in olive oil. Do not over cook.
3. Serve with Marinara Sauce (see Index)

PARISA LORRAINE

Ingredients:
$\frac{1}{2}$ Cup Ham, finely chopped
$\frac{1}{2}$ Cup Lorraine Cheese, grated
$\frac{1}{2}$ Medium Onion, finely chopped
6 Carr's Table Water Crackers

Directions:
1. Combine first 3 ingredients.
2. Spread over crackers.
3. Serve with a Chardonnay.

PORK BARBEQUE

Ingredients:
4-5 Pounds of Pork Roast (Boston Butt)
2 Large Onions, Chopped
2 Bell Peppers, Chopped
2-4 Cloves Garlic, Crushed
Salt
Coarse Black Pepper
Barbeque Sauce, Commercial or Homemade
Still Beer

Directions:
Cook pork in crock pot with water, salt, pepper, and still beer overnight, or until meat falls from bones. Drain, cool, and separate meat from bones. Shred meat and return to crock pot with chopped onion, bell pepper, and garlic. Add enough barbeque sauce and still beer to cover. Adjust spices to suit taste. Cook on low for several hours.
Serve on Hoagie rolls with Cole Slaw.

STEAMED DUMPLINGS
(Pot Stickers)

Ingredients:
$^1/_2$ Pound Lean Ground Pork
2 Oz. Shiitake Mushrooms, chopped
$^1/_4$ Pound Bok Choy, chopped
2 Tbs. Bamboo Shoots, chopped
1 Tsp. Ginger Root, chopped
1 Tbs. Shallots, chopped
1 Tbs. Sesame Oil
1 Tbs. Soy Sauce
$^1/_2$ Tsp. Sea Salt
$^1/_4$ Tsp. Ajinomoto
2 Tbs. Salad Oil to cook
Basic Dough, done in 5" circles

Directions:
1. Chop and combine all ingredients from pork to Ajinomoto.
2. Add to dough circles and pinch up edges.
3. Lightly brown bottoms of dumplings in sesame oil, then cover with water and steam until ready.
4. Serve with dipping sauce (below).

DIPPING SAUCE

Ingredients:
$^1/_4$ Cup Soy Sauce
1 Tbs. Honey
1 Tsp. Rice Vinegar
1 Tsp. Minced Garlic
1 Tsp. Chili Oil
$^1/_2$ Tsp. Fish Sauce
$^1/_2$ Tsp. Wasabe Paste
1 Tbs. Sherry (or Sake)

Directions:
Mix all ingredients together and allow to set for 30 minutes.
Serve with Dumplings.

BIFTECKS TARTARE LAUSANNE

Ingredients:

>1½ Pounds Beef Tenderloin, thoroughly trimmed, and
>ground twice (at home!)
>4 Egg Yolks
>4 Tbs. Cognac*
>4 Tsp. Non-Pareil Capers
>6 Tsp. Shallots, Chopped

>On Deck:
>>Garlic Powder
>>Mixed Herb Seasoning
>>Salt
>>Pepper
>>Lemon Slices
>>Tobasco Sauce
>>Worcestershire Sauce
>>Chervil
>>Hot Pepper
>>Anchovy Paste

Serving suggestions:

As an Entré: Form 4 "bird nests" of ground tenderloin, adding one egg yolk to each, and top with shallots, capers, and cognac to form basic unit. Serve along with the "on deck" seasonings. Each person then adds whatever ingredients they wish, mixes thoroughly with a fork, and enjoys.

As an Appetizer: Mix all basic ingredients together along with whatever spices determined desirable. Have lemon slices "on deck". Serve with small "cocktail" slices of toasted and buttered Pumpernickel bread.

Appropriate Wines:

As an Entré—An estate bottled, aged red burgundy such as a 1982
>Richebourg.

As an Appetizer—A good Brut Champagne, such as a 1983 Dom
>Perignon.

*The cognac eliminates the coating of the hard palate by this meal.

HAMBURGERS À LA GREQUE

Ingredients:

> 1 pound lean ground beef
> $^1/_4$ cup red onions, chopped
> 1 Tsp. Garlic, chopped
> 1 jumbo egg, whipped
> 1 Tbs. dried Basil
> 1 Tsp. dried peppermint
> 1 Tsp. dried thyme
> $^1/_2$ Tsp. coriander
>
> Feta Cheese, sliced
> Yogurt
> Extra Virgin Olive Oil
> Pita bread (Optional), lettuce and tomato (optional)
> Dried dillweed as garnish (optional)

Directions:

1. Whip egg in bowl. Add spices and ground beef.
2. Sauté onions and garlic in olive oil then add to bowl. Mix thoroughly and make into 4 thin patties.
3. Place sliced Feta in the center of each patty, and fold over the sides to seal the cheese in the center.
4. Fry in Extra Virgin Olive Oil (Rare, Please!). Top with Yogurt and Dill Weed, and serve with a good red wine, such as a Demestica.

MACHACADO CON HUEVO

Ingredients:

A. 1¼ Pounds of Beef (Example: rib steaks, sliced ¾" thick)
   2 Beef Bouillon Cubes
   2 Bay Leaves
   "Pinch" of Ground Cloves
   ½ Tsp. Tabasco Sauce

B. ¼ Cup Chopped Bell Peppers
   ¼ Cup Chopped Green Onions
   2 Chopped Jalapeno Peppers
   2 Cloves Garlic, Chopped
   ⅛ Tsp. Course Black Pepper
   ¼ Tsp. Sea Salt
   2 Tbs. Clarified Butter

C. 4 Large/Jumbo Eggs, Whipped in Bowl.
   ¼ Cup Butter
   ½ Tsp. Cumin Powder
   ½ Tsp. Chili Powder
   ¼ Tsp. Cilantro Powder

D. Sour Cream
   Fresh Cilantro Sprigs

Directions:

1. Combine items in section A in about 2 quarts of water and bring to a boil, reduce heat and simmer for 2 hours, until tender. When cooked, remove meat and shred into fine fibers with hands. Set aside. Discard all connective tissue and fat.
2. At the same time, chop peppers, onions, and garlic, and brown in clarified butter. Add salt and pepper. Cook until nearly dry.
3. Combine ingredients in section C and cook in butter while chopping with spatula until pea sized.
4. Add shredded beef to section B vegetables, and stir fry until fairly dry (about 10 minutes). Add egg-spice mixture, mix and top with sour cream and garnish with about 3 sprigs of cilantro per serving. Serves 3 to 4 people.

MEATBALLS BORDELAISE

Ingredients:

A. 1½ Pounds Ground Beef
½ Pound Ground Pork
1 Cup Plain Bread Crumb
2 Jumbo Eggs, whipped in a cup
1 Tsp. Each:
Chervil
Parsley
Thyme
Garlic Powder
Onion Powder
½ Tsp. Each:
Salt
Powdered Bay Leaf
¼ Tsp. Each:
Cayenne Pepper
White Pepper
Black Pepper
Extra Virgin Olive Oil
Clarified Butter

B. Bordelaise Sauce

Directions:

1. Combine all ingredients in "A", mix thoroughly, and allow to equilibrate for 30 minutes in refrigerator.
2. Remove from refrigerator and roll into 36 walnut-sized balls. Brown in a 50/50 mixture of clarified butter and extra virgin olive oil (12 balls at a time). Drain each batch on paper towels and set aside.
3. When all meatballs are done, re-add to frying pan, and cover with water, top with a lid and steam for 20 minutes.
4. Transfer to pan containing Bordelaise Sauce and simmer gently for 20 minutes.
5. Serve with French style green beans with butter and Bouquet Garni Vinegar.
6. A great choice of wine here would be a Pomerol or a St. Emilion, 1984.

PARISA* ROYALE

Ingredients:

    1 Pound Fresh Ground Beef Tenderloin
    1 Cup Grated Alsace-Lorraine Cheese
    $\frac{1}{4}$ Cup Chopped Shallots
    1 Tbs. Garlic Powder
    1 Tbs. Non-pareil Capers
    $1\frac{1}{2}$ Tsp. Chervil
    $\frac{1}{4}$ Tsp. Salt
    $\frac{1}{8}$ Tsp. White Pepper

Directions:

1. Mix all ingredients together thoroughly. Chill for 1 hour.
2. Serve on Carr's King Sized Table Water Crackers.
3. Serve with an Alsatian Gewürztraminer, or Riesling.

Variant: Substitute certified pork for all or part of the beef.

*The original Parisa was created in Castroville, Texas, an Alsatian community since the 1840's.

SIAMBURGERS

Ingredients:

    $\frac{3}{4}$ Pound Lean Ground Beef
    2 Tbs. Chopped Shallots
    $1\frac{1}{2}$ Tbs. Chopped Ginger
    1 Tbs. Chopped Fresh Basil
    1 Tsp. Sea Salt
    $\frac{1}{4}$ Tsp. Coarse Black Pepper
    2 Eggs, whipped in a cup
    $\frac{1}{4}$ Cup Corn Oil
    2 Tbs. Sesame Oil
    French Bread, sliced $\frac{1}{4}$" thick

Directions:

1. Combine first 6 ingredients and allow to marinate for $\frac{1}{2}$ hour. Form 4 oval patties.
2. Dip patties into whipped egg and fry in oil mixture to desired doneness. Serve over bread slices.

SLOPPY JOES

Ingredients:

2 Pounds Lean Ground Beef
2 Large Bell Peppers, Finely Chopped
2 Large Onions, Finely Chopped
2 Cloves Garlic, Finely Chopped
1 Large Can of Tomatoes, Mashed
1 Tbs. Each: Chili Powder, Cumin, Oregano, Worcestershire
Sauce, Tabasco Sauce, and Sea Salt
2 Tbs. Course Ground Black Pepper
2 Tbs. Cooking Oil

Directions:

Fry onion, garlic, and bell pepper in oil until limp. Add ground beef and brown. Add remaining ingredients, cover and simmer for at least 1 hour. Serve on buns, or alternatively, on a corn tortilla topped with a fried egg and grated cheese.

A heavy-bodied beer or ale is good with this meal.

OTHER SUGGESTIONS

Veal Holsteiner
Veal Marsala
Vitello Involuti
Dolmas
Lamb Shish Kebab
Persian Lamb
Rogan Gosht
Medallions of Pork
Pork Satay
Chateaubriand en Bèarnaise
Steak Tampiqueño
Tournedos Rossini

Chapter 8

Cooking poultry is a challenge. Fried to death it is tougher than walnut shells, especially when kept on hot lights for hours in a restaurant or, worse, on an airline.

The first rule is this: cook it, yes, but not over-cook it. It is best when slightly pink in the center.

Marinades do well for poultry, as do dressings (stuffing). Excellent examples are Peking Duck, Turkey with Chestnut Dressing, and Quail with Wild Rice Stuffing.

Finally, always serve good poultry with an appropriate wine. Red, white and rosé all are appropriate, depending upon the meal.

Coq au Vin: a heavy red wine
Turkey: a Tavel Rosé
Chicken/Duck: a crisp Chardonnay

CHICKEN FOUNTAINHEAD

Ingredients:

¾ lb. Chicken tenders,
   tendon removed, and cubed
1 Cup white Wine (Chardonnay)
1½ Tbs. Fresh Ginger, minced
2 Tbs. Chopped Shallots
1 Tsp. Fresh Chopped Garlic
1 Tsp. Dijon Mustard

¼ Tsp. Each: Cayenne Pepper,
   Black Pepper & White Pepper
1 Tbs. Brown Sugar
2 Tbs. Rice Flour Dissolved in
   ¼ cup water
3 Tbs. Cream Cheese to thicken
Extra Virgin Olive Oil

Directions:

1. Sauté chicken in olive oil. Set aside.
2. Sauté ginger, shallots and garlic in same pan, and then add wine, sugar, peppers, and mustard.
3. Add dissolved rice flour and stir. Then add cream cheese.
4. It is mandatory to serve this with a very dry white burgundy such as a Chevalier Montrachet, 1992.

CHICKEN HATER'S CHICKEN TARRAGON

Ingredients:

1 Pound skinless, boneless
   Chicken Breasts
   (tendon removed)
¼ Cup Clarified Butter
¼ Cup Chicken Broth
¼ Cup Chardonnay
3 Chopped Shallots
2 Cloves Garlic, Chopped

2 Tsp. Dried Tarragon, powdered
1 Tsp. Hungarian Paprika
½ Tsp. Worcestershire Sauce
¼ Tsp. Each: Tabasco Sauce,
   Seasoned Salt, White Pepper
½ Pint Sour Cream
1 Tbs. Lemon Juice

Directions:

     Cook chicken lightly in butter, remove from pan and set aside. Add all remaining ingredients except sour cream and lemon juice, and simmer for about 10 minutes. Add sour cream, lemon juice, and return chicken to pan. Stir to mix and serve with remaining Chardonnay. A top quality Chardonnay such as a Montrachet or Puilly-Fume is appropriate (try the 1989's).

NOTE: After flying over 3,000,000 miles, and eating cold, greasy, fried chicken, not to mention 5 years of college fraternity food, one loses virtually all desire for feathered anything. This meal will win you back, as it did me—JEP

CHICKEN TENDERS ANGELICA

Ingredients:

    1 Pound Chicken Tenders, tendons removed

    1½ Cups Mixed Green, Red and Yellow Bell Peppers, Thinly Sliced

    1 Cup Onion, Thinly Sliced

    ½ Tbs. Chopped Garlic

    ¾ Cup Mushrooms, Thinly Sliced

    1 Tsp. Each:

        Oregano

        Basil

        Parsley

        (Note: Preferably use 1 Tbs. each of the fresh picked herbs.)

    ½ Tsp. Each of Black and White Pepper

    ½ Cup Chicken Broth

    ½ Cup Heavy Cream

    Unsalted Butter

    Angel Hair Pasta

Directions:

1. Brown chicken lightly in butter, set aside.
2. Sauté onion, garlic, peppers and mushrooms in butter until limp.
3. Add chicken broth, cream and spices. Simmer until tender and sauce in thickened. Re-add chicken and warm.
4. Serve over Angel Hair Pasta.

DINOSAUR EGGS

Ingredients:

      12 Eggs
      4 Tea Bags
      1/4 Cup Soy Sauce
      2 Star Anise "Flowers"
      1 Tbs. Sugar
      1 Tsp. Sriracha Sauce (or Tabasco Sauce)

Directions:

Add 12 eggs to saucepan containing 2 quarts cold water and bring to a boil. Turn off fire, cover pan, and set aside for 15 minutes. Rinse in ice cold water in a colander, then crack shells by rolling egg with hand on a cutting board until shell is crumbled, but not split.

Add prepared eggs to saucepan containing 2 quarts water, soy sauce, star anise, sugar and hot sauce. Add tea bags and bring to a boil for 5 minutes. Remove tea bags and simmer for 30 minutes longer.

Cover and let stand for 1 1/2 hours. Serve in shell.

OTHER SUGGESTIONS

      Chicken Cordon Bleu
      Chicken Thailand
      Chicken Enchiladas
      Coq au Vin
      Canard ala Orange
      Honey Duck
      Peking Duck
      Turkey in Mole (enchiladas)
      Turkey with Chestnut Dressing
      Turkey Tetrazzini
      Goose with Chestnut Dressing
      Baked Stuffed Quail
      Doves in Wild Rice
      Grouse Smoked and Stuffed with Oysters

Chapter 9

F ish affords good nutrition, plenty of good vitamins
and minerals, and is easy to chew, especially if not
over-cooked.

Ocean fish tend to be better than freshwater fish,
but don't make a generalization here. Inland trout and
the ever-present bluegills are a true pleasure.
Unfortunately, many inland gamefish, such as Northern
Pike, are not particularly good. The occasional walleye
and striped bass make for great table fare.

The following meals bring out the best in fish.
You will enjoy them.

Wines that go with inland fish tend to be dry
(such as a Chardonnay or a White Bordeaux). Wines for
the fish from the oceans tend to be more open.

BOSTON SCROD

Ingredients:

    A. 1 Pound Scrod Filet, cut in 2 pieces
           1/4 Cup Herbal Vinegar, ideally Bouquet Garni
           2 Tbs. Lime Juice
           2 Tbs. Clarified Butter

    B. 1/2 Cup White Wine
           1 Tsp. Capers (non-pareil)
           1/2 Tsp. Caper Liquor
           1/2 Tsp. Sea Salt
           1/2 Tsp. Each:
               Black Pepper
               White Pepper
               Cayenne Pepper
           2 Tbs. Marinade
           2 Tbs. Dry Sherry
           1/2 Cup Cream

    C. 2 Tbs. Flour
           2 Tbs. Clarified Butter

Directions:

1. Place Scrod in vinegar and lime juice to marinate for 1 hour.
2. Add first 8 ingredients of "B" in a saucepan and briefly simmer. Add 2 Tbs. Marinade.
3. Remove scrod from marinade and blot dry. Sauté briefly on each side in melted butter. Do not overcook! Place in a hold-warm oven while completing sauce.
4. Make a roux with flour and additional butter. Heat until thickened then add contents of saucepan. Just before serving, add cream and sherry. Pour over scrod and serve.
5. A good Chardonnay is appropriate with this meal.

COD CURRY

Ingredients:
- A. 1 Pound Cod Filets (or Haddock or other white fish)

- B. Marinade:
  - 2 Tbs. Lemon Juice
  - 1 Tbs. Lime Juice
  - 1 Tbs. Worchester Sauce
  - $\frac{1}{2}$ Tbs. A-1 Sauce
  - 1 Tbs. Maggi Sauce
  - $\frac{1}{4}$ Cup White Wine
  - 2 Tbs. Shallots, finely chopped
  - 1 Tbs. Ginger, finely chopped

- C. 1 Cup Flour
  - $1\frac{1}{2}$ Tbs. Classic Curry Powder (see Index)
  - 2 Eggs, whipped in a bowl

- D. $1\frac{1}{2}$ Cups Peanut Oil
  - 2 Tbs. Sesame Oil

Directions:
1. Combine marinade ingredients. Add Filets and place in refrigerator for 2 hours, turning every 30 minutes.
2. Remove fish from marinade (reserving marinade for sauce), pat dry with towel.
3. Dip filets in whipped egg, then in mixture of flour and curry powder.
4. Fry fish in hot oil mixture.
5. Heat marinade in saucepan and serve with fish.
6. This dish is wonderful with a Gewürztraminer.
7. For a special treat, substitute the 14 spice (extra-hot) curry powder and add a bit of tamarind to the marinade.

COD PROVENÇAL

Ingredients:

1 Pound Cod (Scrod) Filets, Grilled over open flame (brushed
　　with butter)
1 Whole Onion, chopped
3 Cloves Garlic, chopped
2 Cups Fresh Tomatoes, skinned and chopped
1 Cup Red Wine
¼ Cup Pepperoncini, chopped
2 Tbs. Pine Nuts
1 Tbs. Non-pareil Capers
1 Tsp. Fennel
1 Tsp. Rosemary
1 Tsp. Powdered Bay Leaf
⅛ Tsp. Ground Thai Pepper
⅛ Tsp. White Pepper
2 Tbs. Clarified Butter
2 Tbs. Extra Virgin Olive Oil
¼ Cup Sliced Black Olives for Garnish

Directions:

1. Grill fish over open flame, set aside and keep warm. Do not
   overcook.
2. Grind Rosemary and Fennel with mortar & pestle.
3. Add garlic, onion, and peppers to skillet and sauté with
   butter and oil mixture.
4. Add spices and simmer for 3 minutes.
5. Add tomatoes, pine nuts and Capers. Cook until thickened.
6. Place grilled fish on serving platter and top with sauce and
   black olives.
7. Serve with a dry white wine as common to Provence.

CODFISH WITH HOKIE SAUCE

Ingredients:

> 1 Pound Cod (or other white fish) filets
> 2 Tbs. Sesame Oil
>
> Hokie Sauce:
> > 1 10-12 Oz Can Turkey Gravy
> > 1 Tbs. Maggi Sauce
> > 1 Tbs. Shoyu (or Soy Sauce)
> > ½ Tbs. Non-Pareil Capers
> > ½ Tbs. Caper Juice
> > 1 Tsp. Tabasco Sauce
> > 1 Tsp. Worcestershire Sauce
> > 1 Tsp. Ginger Powder (better: fresh ginger)
> > ½ Tsp. Fish Sauce (or Anchovy Paste)

Directions:

1. Combine all ingredients for sauce and simmer for 30 minutes, or until thick and bubbly.
2. Sauté cod filets in sesame oil until soft, but do not over-cook.
3. Pour sauce over filets and serve with a Gewürztraminer or a Chardonnay.

HADDOCK À LA MARSEILLE

Ingredients:

>6 Haddock Filets
>1½ Tbs. Each of Lemon and Lime Juice
>1 Green Bell Pepper, Sliced into long strips
>2 Onions sliced into thin strips, lengthwise
>3 Cloves Garlic, pressed
>6 Roma Tomatoes, peeled and seeded, then cubed
>1 Tbs. Capers
>½ Tsp. Thyme
>½ Tsp. Anise Seed, finely ground in pestle
>1 Cup dry white wine (ideally from Provence)
>¼ Cup Extra Virgin Olive Oil

Directions:

1. Rinse fish and pat dry with paper towel. Marinate in Lemon/Lime mixture for 1 hours, turning 2-3 times, blot dry.
2. Heat 2 Tbs Olive Oil and saute Peppers, Onions, and Garlic until tender. Add Tomatoes, Capers, Spices, and Wine, and cook for 5 minutes.
3. Divide among 6 plates, and top with filets, which have been lightly cooked on the griddle (or broiled) for no more than 3 minutes to the side.
4. Top with mushrooms and cream sauce (below)
5. Serve with a Gewürztraminer or white wine of Provence.

MUSHROOMS AND CREAM SAUCE

Ingredients:

>12 Ounces Oyster Mushrooms, chopped
>1 Tbs. Clarified Butter (low cholesterol: extra virgin olive oil)
>1 Tsp. Sea Salt
>⅛ Tsp. White Pepper
>1 Cup Heavy Cream (low cholesterol: use cream substitute)

Directions:

Sauté mushrooms in butter. Add salt and pepper. Add cream and stir until it thickens slightly. Pour over fish.

HADDOCK FILET WITH FENNEL

Ingredients:

A. 2 Half Pound Haddock Filets
   2 Tbs. Lemon Juice

B. 1 Cup Fennel Bulb,   1 Tsp. Garlic,
      peeled and chopped   chopped or pressed
   $^1/_2$ Cup Water   1 Tsp. Dill Weed
   $^1/_4$ Cup White Wine $^1/_4$ Cup Cream
   $^1/_2$ Tsp. Marjoram   Hungarian Paprika
   1 Tbs. Capers   2 Tbs. Extra Virgin Olive Oil
   1 Tsp. Sea Salt

Directions:

1. Pat filets dry, then rub down on both sides with lemon juice.
2. Combine fennel bulb with next 7 ingredients and simmer, add cream last.
3. Fry fish in olive oil, no more than 5 minutes on each side, the less the better.
4. To serve, place filets on plate and pour sauce over the top. Dust with paprika.
5. Serve with a dry white burgundy, such as a 1989 Montrachet.

RED SNAPPER ORIENTAL

Ingredients:

$^1/_2$ Pound Snapper Filets,
   skin removed & cut into 1" pieces
1$^1/_2$ Tbs. Lemon Juice
$^1/_2$ Tbs. Lime Juice
1 Tsp. Sriracha Sauce
1 Tsp. Ginger Powder
1 Tsp. Wasabe Powder
1 Tbs. Shoyu
1 Cup Plain Breadcrumbs
$^1/_4$ Cup Wheat Germ
2 Jumbo Eggs, whipped in bowl
2$^1/_2$ Cups Corn Oil + $^1/_4$ Cup Sesame Oil

Directions:

1. Marinate fish for 1 hour in mixture of juices and spices.
2. Dip fish in beaten egg, then bread crumb/wheat germ mixture.
3. Fry in oil, but do not overcook. Gold, not brown.
4. Serve with a steamed zucchini and a good Chardonnay.

SALMON ELLA

Ingredients:

> 1-15 Oz. Can Red Salmon, drained (reserving liquid), skin and bones removed
> 1 Tbs. each: Shallots, Ginger, Garlic, Mint Leaf, all chopped
> 1½ Tbs. Clarified Butter
> 1 Tbs. Lime Juice
> 1 Tbs. Soy Sauce
> ½ Tsp. Sea Salt
> ⅛ Tsp. White Pepper
> 1 Tsp. Maggi Sauce
> 1½ Tsp. Tabasco Sauce
> 1 Tsp. Celery Powder
> 1 Tsp. Gumbo Filé
> 1 Tbs. Rice Flour
> 1 Cup Coconut Milk

Directions:

1. Sauté vegetables in butter, add lime juice and spices, and simmer for 30 minutes.
2. Add salmon (chunked) and simmer for 5 minutes.
3. Serve over a bed of rice ("Wild Pecan" rice is particularly good here).
4. White Bordeaux is just lovely with this meal.

Note: J. C. Philpott created this dish!

SALMON FRITTATA

Ingredients:

    A. 1-15 oz. Can Red Salmon, drained (give liquid to cat!)
    B. 6 Eggs
        1 Cup Heavy Cream
        1 Tbs. Rice Flour
    C. 2 Cloves Garlic, chopped
        1/4 Tsp. Each:
          Chervil
          Parsley
          Tarragon
          White Pepper
          Sea Salt
        1/8 Tsp. Each:
          Bay Leaf Powder
          Dill Weed
          Cayenne
    D. On Deck:
          Clarified Butter
          Plain Bread Crumbs
          Romano Cheese

Directions:

1. Lightly whip eggs and cream. Add rice flour and mix thoroughly.
2. Add garlic and spice mixture (C, above) to egg mixture and set aside.
3. Prepare a 10" quiche dish by coating with butter, then bread crumbs.
4. Gently add salmon, then pour egg and spice mixture over top.
5. Bake in moderate (375° F) oven for 30 minutes, or until done.
6. Serve with a high quality Chardonnay. The Creole Chicken-Rice Soup is a good companion dish.

SALMON FOUNTAINHEAD

Ingredients:

Two 1 pound Salmon Filets, rinse (Red Sockeye)

Marinade:
Lemon Juice
Brown Sugar
Honey

Sauce:
10 Oz. Can Crushed Pineapple, drained
2 Fresh Jalapenos, chopped
2 Tbs. Shallots, chopped
2 Tsp. Fresh Cilantro, chopped
2 Tsp. Lemon Juice

Directions:

1. Rub salmon with marinade and leave at room temperature for 1 hour.
2. Broil salmon on grill, basting with marinade (Do Not Overcook!)
3. Serve, topped with sauce.
4. A good Chardonnay wine is best with this meal.

SALMON OMELET

Ingredients:

4 Large-Jumbo Eggs, lightly beaten
$1/2$ Pound Nova Scotia Lox (trimmings cost little compared to whole)
2 Tbs. Shallots, chopped
1 Tsp. Chives
$1/8$ Tsp. White Pepper, Black Pepper & Fresh Marjoram (less if dried)
1 Clove Garlic, chopped
1 Tbs. Lemon Juice
$1/2$ Tsp. Salt
2 Tbs. Clarified Butter

Directions:

Place eggs, shallots, lemon juice, chives and spices in a bowl and mix, beating with a whisk lightly. Melt butter in omelet pan and pour in egg mixture. When nearly done, add finely chopped Lox on one half of egg and fold other half over the top. Serve with Southwestern Cream Sauce (See Index).

SALMON OSCAR

Ingredients:

14-16 Oz. Can Red Salmon (Variant: Smoked Salmon,
especially Nova Lox!).
$^1/_4$ Cup Chopped Green Olive with Pimento
2 Tbs. Shallots, Finely Chopped
2 Tbs. Green Onion, Finely Chopped
$^1/_2$ Cup Plain Bread Crumbs
2 Jumbo Eggs, Lightly Beaten

$^1/_2$ Tsp. Dill Weed
$^1/_2$ Tsp. White Pepper
$^1/_4$ Tsp. Ginger
$^1/_4$ Tsp. Allspice
$^1/_4$ Tsp. Mustard Powder
$^1/_8$ Tsp. Cardamom Powder

$^1/_4$ Cup Heavy Cream

Directions:

1. Clean Salmon, and crumble. Add remaining ingredients and
   set aside in refrigerator for 30 minutes.
2. Form into loaf and bake at 350° F for 35 minute, in pan
   lightly covered with olive oil.
3. Slice into 4 slices, and serve plain or with a Hollandaise
   sauce, if desired.
4. A flinty-dry Chablis, or better, a vintage White Burgundy
   (such as a Pouilly-Fuissé) is a welcome wine.

SALMON PATTIES

Ingredients:

7$\frac{1}{2}$ Oz. Can of Red Salmon, drained, bones and skin removed
$\frac{1}{4}$ Cup Whipping Cream
$\frac{1}{4}$ Cup Plain Bread Crumbs
1 Egg, Whipped
$\frac{1}{8}$ Tsp. Each: Black Pepper, White Pepper, Red Pepper (Cayenne)
$\frac{1}{8}$ Tsp. Sea Salt
$\frac{1}{8}$ Tsp. Thyme
1 Tsp. Capers, plus 1 Tsp. Caper juice (Non-Pareil!)
1 Tbs. Shallots, chopped
1 Clove Garlic, chopped
1 Tbs. Lemon Juice

Directions:

Combine all ingredients in mixing bowl and allow to rest for 15-20 minutes. Form into 4 patties and fry lightly in clarified butter. Serve topped with Southwestern Cream Sauce (see Index).

SALMON QUENELLES

Ingredients:

1 Stalk Celery
$\frac{1}{2}$ Cup Onion
2 Cloves Garlic
1$\frac{1}{2}$ Cups Mushrooms
1 Tsp. Curry Powder
1 Tsp. Hungarian Paprika
1 Tbs. Capers
$\frac{1}{4}$ Tsp. Nutmeg

1 Can Red Salmon, including liquid, but not bones & skin
3 Jumbo Eggs
$\frac{1}{8}$ Tsp. Cayenne
$\frac{1}{4}$ Tsp. Nutmeg
1 Tbs. Lemon Juice
Clarified Butter

Directions:

Combine items in top list and sauté in clarified butter. Add to a blender and chop finely. Add Salmon, eggs, cayenne, salt, and lemon juice. Chop entire mixture finely. Add to well buttered poacher cups and cook until firm.

Serve over toast points, topped with Cream Sauce. This meal is excellent with a dry white Bordeaux.

SCROD SUPREME

Ingredients:

2 One Pound skinless filets
of Scrod or Haddock
1 Tsp. Sea Salt
1 Tsp. White Pepper
2 Tbs. Olive Oil
Juice of ½ Lemon (1 Tbs.)

1 Tsp. Hungarian Paprika
2 Tbs. Chopped fresh Parsley
(or 2 Tsp. Dried)
2 Tbs. Chili Sauce
(the hotter the better!)
1-2 Cloves Garlic, crushed

Directions:

Wipe fish dry with paper towels and rub in salt and white pepper. Coat broiler rack generously with olive oil. Add fish topped with the mixture of spices. Broil for 5 minutes, flip over, and baste with spice mixture. Cook for 5 minutes more. Serve with a white Graves.

THAI OCEAN PERCH

Ingredients:

10-12 Ounces Ocean Perch Filets, skin removed

Soy Sauce Mixture:
1½ Tbs. Soy Sauce, ideally Mirin
½ Tbs. Sriracha Sauce
1½ Tbs. Lemon Juice
½ Tbs. White Wine

2 Tbs. Shallots, chopped
½ Tbs. Dried Ginger (or Kha, if available)
½ Cup Peanut Oil
1 Tbs. Sesame Oil

Directions:

Marinate fish in soy sauce mixture for 1 hour. Remove fish, but reserve liquid. Stir-fry shallots in small amount of the cooking oil, then add the marinade. Heat the cooking oil to about 375 deg. F. and add the filets briefly. Serve on a platter, topped with the marinade mixture. Accompany with snow peas and crab-asparagus soup.
Serve with a nice Malvasia wine.

TRUITE DE REVIERE JENNIFER

Ingredients:

2 Fresh (or fresh frozen) Trout (about 1 pound)

Flour Mixture:
- 1 Cup Flour
- 2 Tbs. White Cornmeal
- 1 Tsp. White Pepper
- $\frac{1}{8}$ Tsp. Cayenne
- $\frac{1}{4}$ Tsp. Nutmeg

Cooking Oil:
- $\frac{1}{4}$ Cup Clarified Butter
- $\frac{1}{4}$ Cup Extra Virgin Olive Oil

Sauce:
- 3 Shallots, finely chopped
- 1 Tsp. Non-pareil Capers
- $\frac{1}{4}$ Cup Sliced Brazil Nuts
- 1 Clove Garlic, Crushed
- $\frac{1}{2}$ Tsp. Ginger
- 1 Tsp. Fresh Mint Leaves
- 1 Tsp. Fresh Cilantro
- $\frac{1}{2}$ Cup Cream
- 1-2 Tbs. White Port or Dry Sherry
- 1 Tsp. Lime Juice

Directions:

Rinse Trout and pat dry with a paper towel. Coat with the flour mixture. Sauté shallots, capers, Brazil nuts, garlic, ginger, mint, and cilantro in 1-Tbs. butter/oil mixture. Add cream, wine, and lime-juice. Cook Trout in oil. Cover with sauce and serve with a CRISP Chardonnay such as a Montrachet or a Charmes.

OTHER SUGGESTIONS

Baked Stuffed Flounder	Crawfish Ettoufée	Sea Trout Amandine
Bon Femme	Finnan Haddie	Seviche
Bouillabaisse	Kippered Salmon	Shad Roe
Cioppino/	Pompano en Papillote	Tempura
Cod Béchamel	Salmon Mousse	

Chapter 10

Shellfish, when not overcooked, is a delight. When cooking, lightly sauté the fish, then set aside. Prepare the remaining ingredients, and then add back the fish to the pot no more than 2 minutes prior to serving.

Oysters, clams, mussels and crawfish are all wonderful when not overcooked. They make delightful soups, rice toppers, and are great in salads.

Crabs and lobsters are most versatile, and can be used in a variety of meals. Crab Thermador and Lobster Newburg are among the house favorites. Our very favorite is a lobster stuffed with crabmeat (please include the tomalley and the coral).

Please do not serve any of these dishes to your Jewish or Muslim friends. These are considered off-limits to them.

BAY SCALLOPS CREPES

Ingredients:

$^2/_3$ Pounds Fresh Bay Scallops
$^1/_2$ Cup Lemon Juice
1 Cup Chopped Mushrooms
2 Tbs. Chopped Shallots
2 Cloves Chopped Garlic
2 Tbs. Chopped Celery
$^1/_2$ Tsp. Cayenne Pepper
$^1/_2$ Tsp. Black Pepper
$^1/_2$ Tsp. White Pepper
3 Tbs. Clarified Butter

Sauce: $^1/_4$ Cup Chablis
$^1/_4$ Cup Heavy Cream
1 Tbs. Sugar
$^1/_2$ Tsp. Powdered Bay Leaf
$^1/_2$ Tsp. Thyme
$^1/_2$ Tsp. Chervil

Directions:

1. Marinate scallops in $^1/_2$ cup lemon juice for $^1/_2$ hour, then drain.
2. Brown mushrooms, shallots, garlic and celery in butter, add spices.
3. Return scallops to pan, warm slightly, and set aside.
4. Combine all sauce ingredients in a saucepan and thicken slightly. Divide in half.
5. Add half of sauce to scallop mixture. Roll this in light crepes.
6. Place rolled crepes in a baking dish and top with remaining sauce.
7. Sprinkle top of crepes with paprika and warm in medium oven.
8. Serve with a moderately sweet Riesling (Spatlese).

COQUELLES ST. JACQUES

Ingredients:

A. 1 Pound Bay Scallops marinated in 2-Tbs. lemon juice for
    2 hours
  4 Shallots, chopped
  $1/2$ Tsp. each: Parsley, Sage, and Thyme
  $1/4$ Tsp. Powdered Bay Leaf
  4 Oz. Fresh Mushrooms, chopped finely
  1 Tbs. Clarified Butter
  $1/4$ Tsp. Sea Salt
  $1/8$ Tsp. each: Red (cayenne) and White Pepper
  1 Cup Chablis

B. 2 Tbs. clarified butter + 2 Tbs. flour, made into a Roux
  $1/2$ Cup Cream
  1 Tbs. Dry Sherry
  1 Tbs. Sugar

Directions:

1. Simmer shallots and spices in Chablis until tender, then add scallops. Drain, reserving liquid, and set aside. Sauté mushrooms in butter, along with salt and peppers. Drain and set aside, reserving liquid (combine liquids).

2. Add cream, sherry and sugar to roux, add reserved liquid and make into a sauce. Add scallop and mushroom mixtures. Place in ramekins, brown under a broiler, and serve with a Gewürztraminer or Spatlese Riesling.

CRAB AND ARTICHOKE DELIGHT

Ingredients:

       1-14 Oz. Can Artichoke Bottoms, drained
       1-6 Oz. Can Lump Crabmeat, picked over
       1 Tbs. Chopped Shallots
       1 Tbs. Heavy Cream
       1 Tbs. Pimento, chopped
       2 Tsp. Cajun 14 Spice Powder (See Index)
       1 Tsp. Dried Chervil
       Clarified Butter (~2 Tbs.)
       Sea Salt (~1 Tsp.)
       Hungarian Paprika (~$\frac{1}{4}$ Tsp.)

Directions:

1. Simmer artichokes in water with sea salt.
2. Sauté shallots and garlic in butter until limp.
3. Sauté crabmeat in butter. Then add cream, spice mixture, and garlic-shallot mix. Simmer, then divide among the artichoke bottoms, and dust with paprika.
4. Serve with a quality Chardonnay.

CRAB CAKES

Ingredients:

  2 6-oz cans of Crabmeat, picked over
  1½ cups Plain Bread Crumbs
  1 Jumbo Egg, Whipped in a Cup
  2 Tbs. All-purpose Flour (used to dredge other ingredients)
  1 Tbs. Capers
  1 Tbs. Dijon Mustard
  1 Tsp. Each: Powdered Bay Leaf, Thyme, Chervil, and
      Worcestershire Sauce
  2 Chopped Shallots
  ½ Tsp. Salt
  ¼ Tsp. Tabasco Sauce
  2 Tbs. Clarified Butter (for Browning)
  ½ Cup Concentrated Chicken Stock (boil down a 10½ oz. Can)
  ½ Cup Cream
  1 Tbs. Caper Liquor
  1 Tsp. Herbal Vinegar
  ⅛ Tsp. Each: White, Black and Red Pepper

Directions:

  Combine first 11 ingredients and form into 4 patties. Dredge in
flour and fry in clarified butter until browned.

  Mix remaining ingredients and make a sauce. Serve with a dry
White Bordeaux such as a 1988 Chateau Haut-Brion.

CRAB EGG FOO YUNG

Ingredients:

$^1/_2$ Pound Crabmeat, ideally Dungeness
$^3/_4$ Cup Bean Sprouts,
$^3/_4$ Cup Bamboo Shoots
4 Green Onions, sliced to 1" length
$^1/_4$ Cup Chopped Mushrooms
2 Tbs. Wood Ears
1 Tbs. Chopped Cilantro
2 Tbs. Soy Sauce
$^1/_2$ Cup Bok Choy, Chopped
1 Tsp. Ginger, chopped
$^1/_2$ Tsp. Celery Powder
$^1/_2$ Tsp. 5 Spice Powder
1 Tsp. Sea Salt.
1 Tsp. Sriracha Sauce.
6 Jumbo Eggs.

Directions:

1. Mix all ingredients thoroughly and cook in frying pan in portions about 5" in diameter. Brown on both sides.
2. Serve with a brown gravy sauce.

CRAB LOUIS

Ingredients:

1 Pound Crabmeat, preferably Dungeness
1 Cup Mayonnaise
$^{1}/_{2}$ Cup Heavy Cream
$^{1}/_{4}$ Cup Picante Sauce
$^{1}/_{4}$ Cup Green Pepper, chopped
2 Tsp. Shallots, chopped
2 Tbs. Green Olives with Pimento, chopped
1 Tbs. Lime Juice
2 Tsp. Hungarian Paprika
$^{1}/_{2}$ Tsp. Worcestershire Sauce
$^{1}/_{2}$ Tsp. Tabasco Sauce
1 Tsp. Capers
1 Tsp. Dijon Mustard
1 Tsp. Horseradish

Garnish: Chives, Cilantro, Avocado, Hard Boiled Eggs, Boston Lettuce, Tomato.

Directions:

1. Pick over crabmeat, removing any leftover shell. Leave in large chunks, if possible.
2. Combine remaining ingredients and gently stir in crabmeat. Chill.
3. To serve, place lettuce leaves on plate, top with crab mixture, avocado slices, hard-boiled eggs, cilantro, chives and chopped tomato.
4. This is wonderful served with a high quality dry white wine, such as a Montrachet.

CRAB THERMIDOR I

Ingredients:

1½ Pounds Crabmeat
2 Cloves Garlic, crushed
½ Cup Breadcrumbs
2 Tbs. Chopped Mushrooms
¾ Cup Cream
2 Eggs, beaten
¼ Tsp. Hungarian Paprika
¾ Tsp. Dry Mustard
¼ Tsp. Salt
1 Tsp. Horseradish
½ Tsp. Tabasco Sauce
1 Tbs. Sherry or Marsala
¼ Tsp. Vanilla Extract
¼ Tsp. Ginger
½ Tsp. Curry Powder
4 Tbs. Clarified Butter

Directions:

1. Sauté crab, mushrooms, garlic and breadcrumbs in 2-Tbs. butter and set aside.
2. Add remaining butter to same pan and combine remaining ingredients. Cook over low heat.
3. Add to crab mixture and transfer to baking dish.
4. Top with more breadcrumbs and grated Parmesan cheese.
5. Bake at 375° F. for 20 minutes.
6. Serve with a white burgundy, such as a Bâtard-Montrachet, 1982.

CRAB THERMIDOR II

Ingredients:

12-16 oz. Crabmeat, picked over thoroughly
$1/4$ cup Chopped Mushrooms
1 Hot Hungarian Red Pepper, seeded, but not deveined, chopped
1 large, or 2 medium Roma Tomatoes, peeled and chopped
2 Shallots (or Green Onions) chopped,
$1/4$ Cup Green Pepper
$1^1/2$ Tbs. Clarified Butter
2 Cloves Garlic
$1/2$ Tsp. Tabasco Sauce
1 Tsp. Chervil
1 Tbs. Lemon Juice
1 Tsp. Salt
$1/4$ Tsp. White Pepper
$1/4$ Cup Cream
2 Tbs. Sherry

Directions:

Combine all ingredients, cooking in melted, clarified butter.
Transfer to 2 individual baking dishes (4, if a side dish) and cover with a
dusting of bread crumbs and brush with melted butter.
Brown in oven for 30 minutes at 350° F.

Serving Suggestions:

Wine: Very Dry Chardonnay
Garnish: Pickled Ginger Slices (available in Oriental groceries)

CRABMEAT AND MUSHROOMS FLORENTINE

Ingredients:

    A. One 4½ Ounce can Lump Crabmeat
        3 Shallots, minced
        1 Clove Garlic, minced
        ½ Tsp. Lemon Juice
        ½ Tsp. Sea Salt
        ¼ Tsp. Tabasco Sauce
        ¼ Tsp. Coarse Black Pepper
        2 Tbs. Clarified Butter

    B. One 14 Oz. Can of Spinach, drained
        2 Tbs. Italian Vinegar
        ¼ Tsp. Anise Seed Powder
        1 Tbs. Clarified Butter

    C. 6 Ounces of Portabella mushroom caps, stems and gills removed.

Directions:

1. Sauté shallots in butter. Add remaining ingredients except crabmeat, and stir. Add crabmeat just before serving.
2. Cook spinach in a saucepan in butter; add vinegar and anise.
3. Soften mushroom caps in microwave oven.
4. Place spinach on plates, top with mushroom caps, add crabmeat stuffing and dust top with Hungarian paprika (optional)
5. Serve with a Gewürztraminer.

CRABMEAT BOMBAY

Ingredients:

    4-5 Oz. Lump Crabmeat (Ideally: Dungeness)
    $1/4$ Cup Heavy Cream
    2 Tbs. Shallots, finely chopped
    $1/2$ Tbs. Honey
    $1/2$ Tbs. Lemon Juice
    $1/2$ Tsp. Garam Masala (see: Index)
    $1/4$ Sea Salt
    $1/8$ Tsp. Hungarian Paprika
    $1/8$ Tsp. Celery Seed
    $1/8$ Tsp. Turmeric
    2 Tbs. Clarified Butter

    Flatbread (Naan, Chapati, or Pita)
    2 Tbs. Clarified Butter

Directions:

1. Sauté shallots until limp in clarified butter; add honey, lemon juice, Garam Masala, sea salt, paprika, celery seed, and turmeric. Mix well.
2. Add cream, mix, and then crabmeat. Cook briefly.
3. Spoon over flatbread, which has been generously coated with butter and heated in oven.

CRABS FOUNTAINHEAD

Ingredients:

    A. 1 Lb. Dungeness Lump Crabmeat, picked over
        3 Tbs. Bouquet Garni Vinegar
        1 Tbs. Lemon Juice
        2 Tbs Sherry
        2 Tsp. Tabasco Sauce or Sriracha Sauce

    B. 2 Tbs. Chopped Shallots
        1 Clove Garlic, Crushed
        $\frac{1}{4}$ Pound Butter

    C. $\frac{1}{4}$ Cup Heavy Cream
        $\frac{1}{2}$ Tsp. Hungarian Paprika

    D. 8 Sliced White Bread, toasted, crusted, and cut on
          a diagonal

Directions:

1. Marinate Crabmeat in items in list A in refrigerator for 2 hours.
2. Melt butter in heavy pan and add shallots and garlic, and brown. Add cream and paprika, mix and bring to a simmer. Add crab mixture and cook only to warm.
3. Serve over toast points along with a good Chardonnay.

CREVETTES PIQUANTE
(Deviled Shrimp)

Ingredients:
    Shrimp:
        1 Pound Medium Shrimp (31-36 to the pound), peeled,
           deveined and rinsed
        $^1/_2$ Cup Plain Bread Crumbs
        2 Large Eggs, whipped in a bowl
        3 Tbs. Clarified Butter

    Sauce:
        2 Tbs. Dijon Mustard
        1 Tbs. Worcestershire Sauce
        1 Tbs. A-1 Sauce
        1 Tbs. Cajun 14 Spice Powder
        3-4 Shallots, finely chopped
        2 Cloves Garlic, crushed
        1-2 Cups Clarified Butter (if necessary)
        1 Tsp. Tabasco Sauce, or more—according to taste
        1 Tbs. Lemon Juice
        2 Cups Beef Stock (or Consumé, in a pinch!)

    On Deck:
        2 Cups Hot Cooked Rice, to which has been added about
          2 Tbs. Clarified Butter

Directions:
1. Dip Shrimp in egg mixture, then in Bread Crumbs
2. Lightly brown in clarified butter, and set aside.
3. Brown the Shallots and Garlic in the clarified butter, adding more if needed.
4. Add all remaining ingredients except lemon juice and simmer until volume is reduced to about $^2/_3$ volume. Add lemon juice and re-add shrimp to re-warm.
5. Serve over rice.

NOTE: This meal deserves a top-quality Chardonnay.

MARINATED SCALLOPS, PLAIN OR STIR FRIED

Ingredients:

   A. ³/₄ Pound Bay Scallops

   B. 2 Tbs. Lemon Juice
      1 Tbs. Mirin
      ¹/₂ Tbs. Shoyu
      1 Tsp. Ginger (or Kha), pressed
      2 Tsp. Coconut Milk
      1 Tsp. Sriracha Sauce

   C. ¹/₂ Tbs. Light Brown Sugar
      1 Tbs. Rice Flour
      1 Tsp. Sesame Oil
      1 Tsp. Nam Pla
      ¹/₄ Tsp. Wasabe Powder
      ¹/₄ Tsp. MSG (Ajinomoto)

   D. Optional: ¹/₂ Cup Vegetable + 1 Tbs. Sesame Oil heated for
      stir-fry.

Directions:

   1. Thoroughly rinse scallops and set aside to drain.
   2. Combine all ingredients in "B" to make marinade. Add
      Scallops and store in refrigerator, mixing several times. Drain
      Scallops, saving marinade, and set aside
   3. Combine ingredients in "C" to make sauce, set aside at room
      temperature.
   4. The scallops may be dipped in the sauce and eaten
      immediately (Japanese style) or may be stir-fried and then
      served with the sauce. They are great both ways.

OYSTERS JACKPOTT

Ingredients:

Sauce:

1 Cup White Wine

2 Cloves Garlic

1 Tsp. Cilantro

1 Tsp. Ginger

2 Tbs. Soy Sauce (or $1^1/_2$ Tbs + $^1/_2$ Tbs Maggi Sauce)

1 Tbs. Oyster Liquor

$^1/_2$ Cup Chicken Stock

Meal:

Drain Oysters, while saving liquor

2 Jumbo Eggs, whipped

Rice Flour

Cottonseed Oil Plus Sesame Oil (4:1)

Cooked Rice

Directions:

1. Build sauce, and liquify in Blender, put in pan, add 1 Tbs. Rice flour, thicken.
2. Dip Oysters in eggs and roll in rice flour
3. Fry in oil, until lightly browned.
4. Serve over rice and top with Sauce.

OYSTERS ROCKEFELLER

Ingredients:
>24 Fresh Oysters
>4 Tbs. Butter
>$\frac{1}{2}$ Cup Minced Spinach
>4 Shallots
>3 Tbs. Chervil
>2 Tbs. Chopped Fresh Celery
>$3\frac{1}{3}$ Tbs. Breadcrumbs
>$\frac{1}{4}$ Tsp. Tabasco Sauce
>$\frac{1}{2}$ Tsp. Salt
>1 Tbs. Anchovy Paste
>$\frac{1}{2}$ Tsp. Thyme
>1 Tbs. Anise Seed
>$1\frac{1}{2}$ Oz. Cognac
>$\frac{1}{2}$ Cup Chablis

Directions:
1. Shuck oysters and reserve liquor. Set aside.
2. Place anise seed on waxed paper and fold paper. Crush anise seed with rolling pin. Add to small pan with cognac and bring to a light boil. Remove from stove and allow to stand for 5 minutes. Filter through a coffee filter into a cooking pan, and rinse twice with the Chablis.
3. Chop chervil, celery, spinach and shallots until fine; add to anise seed extract and simmer, covered for 10 minutes. Add the Tabasco sauce, salt, thyme and anchovy paste. Add butter and wait until totally melted. Add breadcrumbs. Thin with oyster liquor, if necessary.
4. Place half of oyster shells on a cookie sheet and add oysters back to the half shells. Broil oysters in preheated oven at 350° F. for 5 minutes or just until the edges begin to curl. Spread 1 Tbs. of the above sauce and broil for an additional 5 minutes, or until the top is slightly browned. Serve with a Graves or a Montrachet.

PORTABELLA ALLA DUNGENESS

Ingredients:

    A. 4 Portabella Mushroom Caps, stem and gills removed
           (about 6 oz.)

    B. 6 Oz. Dungeness Crab Meat (lumps)

    C. Marinade:
        1 Egg, whipped in a cup
        2 Tbs. Breadcrumbs
        1 Tbs. Dijon Mustard
        1 Tbs. Chopped Shallots
        $1/4$ Tsp. Chervil
        $1/4$ Tsp. Basil
        $1/4$ Tsp. Sage
        2 Tbs. Dry Sherry

    D. Hungarian Paprika
        Romano Cheese

Directions:

1. Combine all ingredients in "C" except Crabmeat. Mix completely, then add crabmeat. Store in refrigerator to 2-3 hours.
2. Distribute marinated crab + marinade among the 4 mushroom caps, and bake at 375° F for 20 minutes.
3. Select any 4 star white burgundy (1989) to go with this meal. If you can find it, try a Vaudesir, as it is a good buy.

SHRIMP TOAST

Ingredients:

$^1/_4$ Pound Shrimp, peeled and deveined
1 Jumbo Egg, whipped in a cup
1 Tbs. Shallot, chopped
$^1/_2$ Tsp. Fresh Ginger
$^1/_2$ Tsp. Kha (Galanga)
1 Tbs. Rice Flour
1 Tsp.Nam Pla (Fish Sauce)
$^1/_2$ Tsp. Sea Salt
2 Tsp. Poppy Seeds (Optional)
6 Slices White Bread, crusts removed and cut into 4 square
    quarters
2 Jumbo Eggs, shipped in bowl, to dip toast before adding
    poppy seeds
1-Quart vegetable oil plus 1 Tbs. Sesame Oil heated to 375° F.

Directions:

1. Combine all ingredients; shrimp to salt, in blender and mix to a fine paste.
2. Spread shrimp mixture on one side of bread squares and dust with Poppy Seeds, if desired.
3. Add to hot oil (shrimp side down) and brown lightly, invert and brown briefly. Remove to warm serving dish.
4. Garnish with cilantro leaves and/or onion brushes (if desired).
5. Dip into Shoyu or even a Sweet and Sour Sauce if you wish, but it does extremely well on its own.
6. Goes well with Champagne!

THAI CRAB FRITTATA

Ingredients:

8 Jumbo Eggs, whipped in a bowl
1 Cup Bean Sprouts
$1/4$ Cup Heavy Cream
$1/2$ Cup Crabmeat, ideally Dungeness
$1/2$ Cup Chopped Celery, cooked
$1/2$ Cup Oyster Mushrooms, chopped
1 Tbs. Chopped Ginger
1 Tbs. Chopped Fresh Cilantro
2 Tbs. Soy Sauce
2 Tbs. Coconut Milk
1 Tbs. Thai Peppers, finely chopped
$1/4$ Tsp. Vanilla Extract
1 Tbs. Romano Cheese
$1/2$ Tsp. Hungarian Paprika
Unsalted Butter
Plain Breadcrumbs

Directions:

1. Beat eggs until blended, add cream and vanilla and mix well.
2. Coat a 9" pie pan or quiche dish with clarified butter, then add breadcrumbs to coat evenly.
3. Add chopped ingredients, then egg and cream mixture.
4. Sprinkle top with Romano cheese and paprika.
5. Bake for 25 minutes at 375° F., or until browned and solid in the center.

THAI SCALLOPS

Ingredients:
>³/₄ Pound Bay Scallops, rinsed and drained
>1 Cup Coconut Milk
>3 Tbs. Furious Yellow Sauce
>2 Tbs. Fresh Peppermint Leaves
>1 Tbs. Shallot, minced
>1 Tbs. Fresh Ginger, minced
>1 Tbs. Tamarind, extracted in ¹/₄ cup white wine
>1 Tsp. Sea Salt
>Sesame Oil

Directions:
1. Sauté shallots and ginger in sesame oil until soft.
2. Add tamarind extract, peppermint, hot sauce, coconut milk and salt.
3. Two minutes before serving add scallops, stirring. Do not overcook scallops!
4. Serve with a Gewürztraminer or Chardonnay.

OTHER SUGGESTIONS

"Buster Crabs" (soft shell crabs), either broiled or fried
   (rolled in rice, Japanese style)
Clam Fritters
Clams in Spanish Rice
Crabmeat Vinaigrette
Curried Oysters
Devils on Horseback
Hangtown Oyster Fry
Lobster Stew a la Boston
Lobster Thermidor
Mussels in Marinara
Oysters Florentine
Scallops Provençale
Shrimp de Jonghe
Shrimp Tempura

Chapter

11

Whether it is before the meal, during the meal, or after the meal, cocktails have been an American tradition since Colonial times.

Desserts are also a sing-along to fine cuisine, and often embody the cocktail as part of their fare.

The reader is referred to the many cookbooks devoted to these for concepts. This section is (as usual) limited to originals that are user-friendly to the folks like you and me with store-bought teeth.

We do have a few contributions to this category. These were created in the early 1970's, and today are greatly appreciated.

COCKTAILS & DESSERTS

BIENENSTICHER
(Bee Stinger)

Ingredients:

 1½ Ounces Barenjager (formerly: Barenfang)
 1½ Ounces White Crème de Menthe
 Twist of Lemon

Directions:

 1. Store all ingredients in refrigerator prior to mixing.
 2. Serve in stemmed glass over ice.

COCO POCO LOCO

Ingredients:

 2 Mature Coconuts, eyes opened and drained. Save juice.
 ¼ Cup Rose's Lime Juice
 3 Shots of Tequila, such as sombrero Negro, or Conmeritivo
 1 Shot Triple Sec

Directions:

 1. Shake all liquid ingredients over ice, and fill coconuts using a funnel.
 2. Add a fragrant flower to one of the "eyes" and a straw to a second "eye".
 3. After finishing drink, break the coconuts, shred the "meat" and store for other nice dishes.

DAMN-THE-WEATHER COCKTAIL

Ingredients:

 1 Oz. Dry Gin (Tanqueray)
 ½ Oz. Sweet Vermouth (Martini & Rossi)
 ½ Oz. Orange Juice
 1 Tsp. Orange Curacao

Directions:

 Shake over ice, strain into cocktail glass and serve.

FRENCH "75" COCKTAIL

Ingredients:

> Juice from 1 Lemon
> 2 Tsp. Powdered Sugar
> 2 Oz. Gin
> 1 Ice Cube
> Dash of Angostura Bitters
> Champagne to fill 12 Oz Glass

Directions:

> Shake with ice, strain and pour into a cocktail glass. Top with lemon slice, orange slice, and maraschino cherry. Serve with a straw.

GLÖGG

Ingredients:

> 3 Liters Burgundy
> 750 ML. 100 Proof Bourbon
> 20 each: Cardamom Seeds, Cloves, and Almonds
> 2 Cups Sugar
> 2 Cinnamon Sticks
> 1 Pound Box of Raisins

Directions:

> Combine ingredients, bring to a light boil, ignite (to burn off almond oil), cover to extinguish and then transfer to a 1 gallon jug and store for 2 weeks.
> Strain into individual mugs and microwave until hot and you have the traditional Swedish Christmas Drink

CHRISTMAS RAISIN PIE

> Separate the raisins from the rest of the ingredients in the Glögg recipe and use to make a baked pie or several fried pies. Delicious!!

KIR

Add 1 Tsp. Crème de Cassis (slowly and gently) to a glass of dry white wine (Chardonnay). Serve with a twist of lemon peel.

KIR ROYALE

Follow basic recipe for KIR, except substitute Champagne for white wine.

PINEAPPLE PLEASURE FOR TWO

Ingredients:
>1 Mature Pineapple
>3 Shots of High Quality Rum
>$1/4$ Cup Coconut Milk

Directions:
>1. Slice top off pineapple about 1 inch below the crown. Notch top to allow for 2 straws.
>2. Scrape pulp with a spoon and place in a blender along with juice.
>3. Add 3 shots of rum, $1/4$ cups coconut milk and ice. Mix thoroughly.
>4. Add mix to pineapple, seal top back on with toothpicks. Add 2 straws to the notches and enjoy cheek-to-cheek.

STRAWBERRIES VICTORIA

Ingredients:
>1 Pint Strawberries (the smaller the berry the better!)
>2 Tbs. Butter melted in pan
>2 Tbs. Brown Sugar
>1 Tbs. Corn Starch
>2 Tbs. Sherry
>$1/3$ Cup Heavy Cream
>$1/4$ Tsp. Mace
>
>4 Slices Cake (a fluffy, vanilla, lemony cake)
>4 Scoops Vanilla Ice Cream
>Whipped Cream
>Maraschino Cherry Halves, or Fresh Bing Cherry Halves

Directions:
1. Slice berries lengthwise into 4 or 5 slices
2. Add brown sugar and cornstarch to melted butter and dissolve. Add mace and sherry. Mix and add cream, stir thoroughly, then add strawberry slices, stirring until berries are soft. Serve over cake with ice cream. Pour some sauce over ice cream.
3. Top cakes with whipped cream and cherry halves.
4. Serve with sparkling wine with 1 small strawberry in each glass. A good choice is a German Sekt or an Asti Spumanti.

TARPLEY TORNEDO

Ingredients:
>4 Shots Rum
>2 Shots Cocktail Sherry
>Juice of $1/2$ Lime
>Juice of 1 Orange
>2 Tbs. Maraschino Cherry Juice

Directions:
>Mix all ingredients together with ice.
>Mix 50:50 with tonic.
>Serve in a coconut shell

TIO GIORGIO COCKTAIL

Ingredients:
>1 Shot of Campari
>1 Shot of Dry Vermouth (Martini and Rossi)*
>1 Tsp. of Pernod
>Ice

Directions:
>Shake Campari and Vermouth over ice and strain into cocktail glass. Slowly pour Pernod over top. Serve with an Italian cigar (such as a Parodi)

Comment:
>This drink was created by my late uncle, George. M. Philpott, Sr. This drink is extremely popular with just about anybody who tries it, especially those of Italian extraction. Uncle George was a bon-vivant who led a life of 90 years of international travel and fine cuisine, and ran his own business for over 50 years.
>*I introduced Dr. Luciano Martini to this fine drink.*

TOP OF THE ROCK

Ingredients:
>2 Shots of Brandy
>2 Shots of Rum
>2 Shots of Gin

>Juice of 3 Oranges
>2 Shots of Rose's Lime Juice
>1 Shot of Grenadine

Directions:
>Serve with ice, mint sprig, cherry and lime slice.

OTHER SUGGESTIONS

>Bananas Foster
>Benedictine and Brandy (layered!)
>Cherries Jubilee
>Greek Stinger
>Kahluah
>Mai Tai Cocktail
>Shillelagh
>Zombie

Postscript

I sincerely hope that these recipes will be as beneficial to you as they were to me. They are time tested, and "mouth tested". I have managed to eat well during the losses, and I trust that you will do so as well.

Should you have any recipes that you consider to be beneficial to anyone in our position, please send them to me. I will be most honored to acknowledge the sources in the next edition of this cookbook.

I have shared these recipes with many friends and relatives who have gone through what I did. My goal is to make the transition that each of us went through easier on those with similar problems.

Most sincerely,

John E. Philpott, Ph.D.

Weights

U.S.A. STYLE	**METRIC STYLE***
1 Dram = 60 Grains (of wheat)	3.75 Grams
8 Drams = 1 Ounce	30 Grams
8 Ounces = ¹/₂ Pound	¹/₄ Kilogram
16 Ounces = 1 Pound	¹/₂ Kilogram

Measures

U.S.A. STYLE	**METRIC STYLE***
¹/₈ Teaspoon = 7.5 Minims (Drops)	¹/₂ Milliliter
¹/₄ Teaspoon = 15 Minims	1 Milliliter (1 c.c.)
¹/₂ Teaspoon	2 Milliliters
1 Teaspoon	4-5 Milliliters
3 Teaspoons = 1 Tablespoon = ¹/₂ Ounce	15 Milliliters
4 Tablespoons = ¹/₄ Cup = 2 Ounces	60 Milliliters
1 Cup = 8 Ounces = 1 Glassful	240 Milliliters
2 Cups = 1 Pint = 16 Ounces	480 Milliliters or +/- ¹/₂ Liter
2 Pints = 1 Quart = 32 Ounces	960 Milliliters = +/- 1 Liter

*These equivalents are based upon the standards of the U.S.P./N.F., and are "close enough" to validity to be acceptable for preparation of pharmaceuticals, let alone culinary preparation.

Index